I0125228

Community Psychoanalysis

This book delves into the history, current status, and possible future directions of psychoanalysis in the community, outside the traditional consulting room.

This book begins by digging into the individualistic origins of psychoanalysis and the clear definitions around what counts as psychoanalysis and what does not, even to this day. It also explores what has remained constant even as psychoanalysis has splintered into many schools of thought. Rather than rejecting individualistic thinking entirely, Altman investigates how a mix of individual- and community-focused work has been effective in various international settings and the role that the arts can play in informing psychoanalytic practice. In pursuit of the new doors that open as psychoanalysis expands in relational directions, this book considers a range of clinical programs that have recently evolved in non-traditional contexts: in schools, in the streets, and in religious and spiritual communities. With access to new and non-traditional modes of understanding and intervention, new possibilities become thinkable.

With international examples of successful community work and drawing on Altman's extensive clinical experience, this is key reading for psychoanalysts and psychotherapists wanting to explore community practice.

Neil Altman is the author of *The Analyst in the Inner City: Race, Class, and Culture through a Psychoanalytic Lens, White Privilege: Psychoanalytic Perspectives*, and *Psychoanalysis in an Age of Accelerating Cultural Change: Spiritual Globalization*. He is a member of the Board of Directors of Harlem Family Services, New York, N.Y.

Community Psychoanalysis

'This is the badly needed definitive textbook, an inspiration for every student of Psychoanalysis in the Community. Altman fills a need for Departments of Psychology, Psychoanalytic Institutes and nationwide courses in Community Applications of Psychoanalysis. Lucidly explaining the origins of psychoanalytic work in communities, Altman begins with Freud's free clinics and ends with modern theories of group interactions, group psychological processes, and connects us with nonlinear processes at work unseen and seldom appreciated by those of us working one on one in private offices. A tour de force, written boldly and honed by real-life work in the streets and public spaces of the world. A masterpiece.'

Gilbert Kliman, MD, *recipient of the Janusz Korczak award for world's best book concerning the nurture and well-being of children, Academy of Child and Adolescent Psychiatry's Rieger Award, APSA's Humanitarian Award, APSA's Freud Award, IPA's 2025 award for psychoanalytic research influencing other fields*

'One of the most valuable contributions of *Community Psychoanalysis*, which aims to veer the profession away from its predominantly individualistic orientation, is the hard-won insight that communities are not undifferentiated groups, just as individuals can hardly be autonomous and autotelic. If people are singular entities, so are communities, Altman argues powerfully, paving the way for a psychoanalysis in the community that considers intrapsychic dynamics in the necessary context of social dynamics. Magisterial in its overview of the translations and adaptations of European psychoanalysis circulating in an international frame, the work is incisive and pragmatic in defining what psychoanalysis is, what the critical stakes of community psychoanalysis are, and what the discipline's very survival depends on. Altman proves himself a virtuoso analyst in the inner city, yet again, and additionally a historian of the social dimensions of psychoanalysis from its inception.'

Ankhi Mukherjee, *University of Oxford, Author of* Unseen City: The Psychic Lives of the Urban Poor

'*Community Psychoanalysis: Bringing the Individual and the Communal Together* accomplishes what it sets out to do. It has a breadth, scope, and historical focus that bridges global and national events. The push for community psychoanalysis continues to be a challenge, yet there are initiatives that may yet yield greater results. This book will certainly contribute to moving this effort forward.'

Luz Towns-Miranda, PhD, *Postdoctoral Program in Psychotherapy and Psychoanalysis, New York University*

'Altman's groundbreaking book shatters the boundaries of traditional psychoanalysis, charging the field to confront its own exclusivity and social blind spots. In a world where the social matrix shapes every psyche, Altman urges us to "take the red pill"—to see how power, community, and context pulse through every analytic encounter. Challenging the old model of the private office and high fees, he envisions a vibrant, flexible "community psychoanalysis" that lives in the real world, embracing diversity, unpredictability, and group dynamics. With passion and urgency, Altman demands a psychoanalysis that listens deeply, adapts boldly, and works for all, not just the few.'

Rev. Sheila P Johnson, MPS, LP, *Chair and President,*
Harlem Family Services, Inc.

Community Psychoanalysis

Bringing the Individual and
the Communal Together

Neil Altman

Routledge
Taylor & Francis Group

LONDON AND NEW YORK

Designed cover image: Getty Image © FangXiaNuo

First published 2026
by Routledge
4 Park Square, Milton Park, Abingdon, Oxon OX14 4RN

and by Routledge
605 Third Avenue, New York, NY 10158

Routledge is an imprint of the Taylor & Francis Group, an informa business

© 2026 Neil Altman

The right of Neil Altman to be identified as author of this work has been asserted in accordance with sections 77 and 78 of the Copyright, Designs and Patents Act 1988.

All rights reserved. No part of this book may be reprinted or reproduced or utilised in any form or by any electronic, mechanical, or other means, now known or hereafter invented, including photocopying and recording, or in any information storage or retrieval system, without permission in writing from the publishers.

For Product Safety Concerns and Information please contact our EU representative GPSR@ taylorandfrancis.com. Taylor & Francis Verlag GmbH, Kaufingerstraße 24, 80331 München, Germany.

Trademark notice: Product or corporate names may be trademarks or registered trademarks, and are used only for identification and explanation without intent to infringe.

British Library Cataloguing-in-Publication Data
A catalogue record for this book is available from the British Library

ISBN: 978-1-041-11691-2 (hbk)
ISBN: 978-1-041-09773-0 (pbk)
ISBN: 978-1-003-66114-6 (ebk)

DOI: 10.4324/9781003661146

Typeset in Optima
by codeMantra

To all those who have worked so diligently, tirelessly, and selflessly to get Harlem Family Services off the ground, striving to meet, at last, the mental health needs of a grossly underserved but nonetheless vibrant community: Sheila Johnson (our leader and inspiration), Gil Kliman (for countless years of unmatched service), Michael Connolly (without whom this project would have died on the vine), Lou Pansulla, Paula Kliger and many, many, others. You have enabled me, so late in my career, to do the work that should have been more highly prioritized all along.

To my beloved children: Lisa, Amanda, and Marcel

To Jillian, who somehow makes her own important contribution to Community Psychoanalysis while keeping the home fires burning.

Contents

Preface

Sigmund Freud made a towering intellectual and clinical contribution, historic and transformative. Freud also very jealously protected his nearly sole right to revise his theory and technique. He was a very controlling person, to the detriment of the long-term viability of the transformative impact of psychoanalysis. He innovated brilliantly and extensively but stood in the way of his followers who wanted to depart from, or even elaborate in their own way on, his theory and practice. More than a century on, the psychoanalytic edifice he built stands, but in need of renovation for the sake of the ongoing relevance of psychoanalysis as the world evolves. The stakes are high: to analysts, a sense of identity, to the general public, the accessibility of our services, the credibility of our theory, and our responsivity to changing circumstances and to crises.

In this book, I suggest that psychoanalysis would benefit from revising some of the more peripheral elements without which the core could survive in a more viable form. Freed from the particularities of Freud's need to establish his credibility among Vienna's *fin-de-siècle* medical establishment, I suggest we can become more accessible and more responsive to more people of different times and places.

My premise is that psychoanalysis as it stands would benefit from being more inclusive and accessible. I refer to a more inclusive and accessible version of psychoanalysis as "Community psychoanalysis", departing from an individualistic bias from which Freud himself frequently departed but which has come to seem a psychoanalytic *sine qua non*. In this book I offer some thoughts on moves that have been made in this direction and how we can continue down that path.

Many of us think of "community" as an entity separate from its constituent elements. In the human world, people are individual entities, so are communities. Group psychoanalysis or Community psychoanalysis is about the functioning of collectives of people. On the margins are those who study the hidden, underground, interconnections between entities that appear to be separate, discrete from a perspective above ground. The underground perspective reveals obscure and all-encompassing connections. In a forest, from above-ground, trees are discrete entities. From underground, where one can see the fungal networks through which trees and other plants interact and communicate, they form one entity (Sengupta, 2022).

Due to the particularities of the evolution of psychoanalysis, individual people have been regarded as discrete entities, albeit with unconsciousness. In this book, I propose to take a look from underground, where we see communities. After all, psychoanalysis is all about what is underground.

Let's start digging.

Nearly 90 years after the death of Sigmund Freud, psychoanalysis is challenged to speak to rapidly changing cultures around the world. There are new generations of therapists and patients, rapidly emerging aspirations and forms of distress and discontent, new ways of making meaning of lives. This book addresses one way in which I think psychoanalysis marginalizes itself, having remained entrenched in a niche, accessible mostly to the affluent or to intellectuals. I propose that this state of affairs results from an outmoded form of individualism, plucking people out of their social contexts, insisting that they lie on a couch, alone, in a private office, cut off from the worlds in which they live. I advocate taking account of the community, the communities, in which our patients are embedded, sometimes including people from those communities, in full-fledged psychoanalyses. I call this "Community psychoanalysis", to be defined in more detail as we proceed.

To be sure, some people benefit from the privacy and the quiet of private offices. Others may feel that what brings them to seek help is all about their social relationships and entanglements, with family, with children and parents, with their communities, with the broader society. There's not enough room on the couch for all those people!

This book is an inquiry into the individualistic basis for the theory and practice of psychoanalysis, a bias that is taken for granted by those who are most immersed in the field and that I will argue in critical respects has led the field astray. Those who have spent years and decades in the field have grown accustomed to focusing on the individual isolated from the context of other people, including specific human communities. This focus on the individual has been justified as required for scientific objectivity, but, adopted uncritically, it situates the field in a long-standing Eurocentric perspective that builds in blindspots alongside, but also undermining, a commitment to making blindspots visible. (One huge blindspot has to do with the undeniable presence of another person, the analyst, in the room, with his or her own personality and blindspots.) Those who have not spent years immersed in psychoanalytic tradition may be more open minded about biases that are deeply embedded in the field, productive in many respects, and also, perhaps under the radar, leading the field astray in other fundamental respects. A fundamental aim of this book is to facilitate perspective on the individualism that has shaped the field, noting the way it has entered the DNA of our concepts and ways of working, and to imagine how the field might look if it were more communitarian. Read as a whole, Freud was clearly as interested in social aspects of human life (e.g. Civilization and its Discontents, or Moses and Monotheism) as he was in intrapsychic, mental life. As a clinician, however, he was a doctor of his time, a one-on-one healer, except when it came to children (Little Hans was treated via his father and always kept the family context in mind). He also departed from his individualism by restricting his one-on-one approach to the "technical" relationship (Lipton, 1979). After hours, so to speak, he dined with his patients and went on hikes with them. He did hypnosis with his patients. He laid on hands and participated in experimental séances (Zeavin, 2018). Clearly, Freud could depart from his otherwise strictly maintained anonymity. Given the tenuousness of his position as a Jewish physician, one of the first at his time and place, he was being especially careful to behave as a proper physician according to the norms at the time. A good deal of what followed in the psychoanalytic history we are about to review can be seen as Freud's followers trying to shake themselves free of unnecessary rigidities, many of which entailed individualistic eccentricities like the couch.

I want to be clear that my goal is not thereby to eliminate individualism from psychoanalysis. Rather, I seek to find a non-exclusionary way for individualism and communitarianism to coexist, by questioning and perhaps eliminating generally unnecessary practices, such as sitting behind the couch, or avoiding responses to direct questions.

Along the way, I will note and reflect on how the traditional psychoanalytic "frame" is necessary in some respects and counterproductive in others. Some aspects of a frame are necessary in order to maintain boundaries between the patient and the analyst, to protect the patient from exploitation, and to keep the focus on the patient's needs. At the same time, a frame devoted to maintaining an unrealistic "objectivity" (via "abstinence" and "anonymity") might be inconsistent with therapeutic aims. The analyst must recognize that some aspects of his or her personal involvement are necessary for the empathy and limit setting which are essential to therapeutic action, and not inconsistent with prevention of exploitation. By the time we get to this book's conclusion, we will be making an effort to disentangle some of these threads in the course of rethinking a framework for analytic work in the patient's best interest.

I note a splitting off of certain aspects of therapeutic action of psychoanalysis from other aspects, associated with, and reinforcing, a splitting, or splintering in the field. Schools of thought in psychoanalysis tend to emphasize primarily insight, primarily enactment, and/or primarily resumption of stalled development. We cannot seem to agree on what, exactly, our priorities are as to what we are doing, or trying to do, or trying not to do. Hovering over these discussions is the question of what, if anything, *is* essentially psychoanalytic. What are the necessary and sufficient factors that make a theory or technique "psychoanalytic"?

Mitchell (1988) divided psychoanalytic theories or schools of thought into those based in a beast metaphor and a baby metaphor. The beast metaphor is implicit in the idea that, in the end, "where id was, ego shall be". This transformation is generally thought to occur via insights activated by inter-pretation. The baby metaphor is associated with an emphasis on what Kohut and his followers thought of as normal narcissistic needs, like idealization, mirroring, and twinship. This model of therapeutic action tends to focus on the evolution of the analytic relationship in such a way as to recognize and address needs that were and are unmet, thus stalling development. Unneces-sary abstinence can reinforce this potentially pathogenic pattern.

Splintering in the field is reflected in a one-sided emphasis on verbaliza-tion and insights as opposed to corrective emotional experiences within the analytic relationship, with and/or without verbalization. Emphasis on enact-ment within the analytic relationship tends to focus on episodes of "impasse and outburst" (Mitchell, 1997, pp. 53–59) in which the analytic relation-ship concretizes ongoing stuck points in development in the form of stuck points in resolving analytic impasses. The analyst tends to get stuck too, with the patient, so that an interpersonal negotiation, in words and/or nonverbal action, becomes necessary. Templates for "moving on" in and out of impasses give rise to templates for new and useful flexibility in interpersonal interac-tions in the "real world". These days, most analytic theorists make room for both verbalization and enactment but prioritize one or the other by conceiv-ing of one as preparatory to, or facilitative of, the other or by conceiving of one dynamic or the other as more truly or essentially psychoanalytic than the other.

Winnicott (1971) and his followers (e.g. Phillips 1993; Ghent, 1991), col-lectively known as the Middle Group tried to transcend this splitting by means of the concept of paradoxical coexistence in "transitional" space. We will see the usefulness of this approach when we come to consideration of the envi-ronment (physical and/or psychological) as implicated, psychoanalytically, in psychological impasses and resolutions. In general, this approach allows us to avoid fruitless impasses around questions as to whether Community psy-choanalysis is *really* psychoanalysis.

Finally, it is not possible to draw a hard and fast line between individ-ual psychoanalysis and Community psychoanalysis. There are a number of potential overlaps. There are also many kinds of communities, from families, to work groups, to municipalities, to neighborhoods, and more. When an individual seeks out psychoanalysis, it is generally because of felt distress which can be linked to a sense of conflict or dissatisfaction or personal fail-ure. As an inquiry unfolds it may start to appear that community-based or sys-temic issues in the family or at work are contributory to the person's distress. Or a family or work issue may appear to touch off a long-standing personal, intrapsychic conflict. In such cases there may be a need for some form of inte-gration between/among individual and/or systemic and /or community-based issues. Clinical judgment may be needed to prioritize whether and how to approach including a family member, a spouse, or an entire family, in an indi-vidual psychoanalysis or when and how to have sessions with an individual in the context of a family- or community-oriented therapy. These are complex choices and should not be driven by a *priori* commitments to one or another sort of theory-driven frame, i.e. who should be in the room (*only* an individual or only a family), or where the session should take place (e.g. sessions *must* be in a private office).

The Organization of This Book

In the first part, somewhat spread throughout the book, we will consider the history of Community psychoanalysis from Freud through the most recent iterations triggered by the COVID pandemic and its aftermath. We will look at how these forms of Community psychoanalysis emerged and evolved and the psychoanalytic politics associated with this evolution. We will look at the multifarious forms Community psychoanalysis has taken, where and when it has been practiced, and future prospects. We will look at the psychoanalytic community itself and how migration and exile have affected the interactions between analysts and communities.

In the second part, we will look at the evolution of psychoanalytic theory, particularly the recent emergence of relational theories. I include here systems theories, family systems theory, nonlinear dynamic systems theory, and group analysis, and their interaction with or merger with Community psychoanalysis. Along the way we will have occasion to try to specify what makes a theory or a practice "psychoanalytic" and how inclusive that designation should be.

Finally, we will consider the arts, specifically literary arts, as potentially psychoanalytic, even as Community psychoanalytic, interventions. We will consider the arts as revelatory in a way that links them in specific ways with psychoanalysis.

Introduction

A History of Community Psychoanalysis

What Is Community Psychoanalysis?

In the absence of a way to articulate the paradoxical coexistence of seemingly alternative units of analysis, i.e. the individual and the group, the idea of Community Psychoanalysis may seem oxymoronic. Most of us have no trouble feeling like individuals who are also members of (multiple) groups. The contradiction arises in the context of scientific psychology, specifically psychoanalysis that seeks to separate, definitively, the objective, dispassionate, observing, analyst from the passionate, experiencing, patient, wracked, shipwrecked, deep into subjectivity. How can the analyst be portrayed as simultaneously a dispassionate observer-scientist *and* a deeply involved participant in a relationship? In the popular imagination, the psychoanalyst appears as captured in the New Yorker-cartoon stereotype of the analytic couple, or rather the analysand on the couch, the analyst behind him or her, out of sight, the two in splendid, though ridiculous, isolation from each other. Their human commonality, the community in which they are embedded, appears nowhere in the picture. Where does this stereotype come from? As with many caricatures, is there a grain of truth in this one?

In Such Cartoons the Analyst as a Co-Participant Is Noted and Ridiculed

Over the years, it has sometimes been noted that Freud himself did not demand such a rigorous setting requiring such thorough-going efforts at detachment and anonymity. He went for walks in the woods with patients and shared meals with them. As pointed out by Lipton (1979), however, Freud made a distinction between a technical relationship with anonymity and neutrality in mind and a non-technical, personal relationship outside of strictly defined sessions. Some modern-day analysts in the Kleinian tradition (e.g. Joseph, 1998) have raised the stakes in this conversation by linking the maintenance of an interpretive stance to a therapeutically necessary "survival" (Winnicott, 1971) of patient attacks on the analytic "frame", derived from the death instinct (Joseph, 1998). To compromise on the rigor of the anonymity and

DOI: 10.4324/9781003661146-1

neutrality of the standard setting was to allow the destruction of the analysis itself. Meanwhile, analysts in both Kleinian (Alvarez, 1992) and Freudian (Stone, 1961) traditions pointed out that an overly strictly maintained frame might create its own interferences with an analytic process. Space for a more flexible procedure was sometimes reserved for certain categories of patients, diagnostically defined, or because of their special needs. Freud distinguished between the "pure gold" (Freud, 1919) of psychoanalysis and the more or less alloyed procedure of "psychotherapy". In some cases, Freud himself had called for all psychoanalytic institutes to sponsor free or low cost clinics (Danto, 2005); all the institutes in Europe had done so, until the Nazis drove out the analysts of Europe in the late 1930s. Refugee analysts, once in the safe harbor of the United States, for the most part retreated into private offices (Jacoby, 1983); thus, the bifurcation of the "community" and the "office" became especially sharply delineated in the United States. In England, this bifurcation was less polarized as the Tavistock institute, a major center of psychoanalytic training and practice, especially with children and adolescents, became part of the British National Health Service. In the post-war United States the Community Mental Health movement, with some government funding, drew some psychoanalytically inclined clinicians into the public sector (Altman, 1995, 2010; Pine, 1985). With time, psychoanalytically oriented therapists in private as well as public settings practiced with more technical freedom but often careful to limit the scope of what they were doing by calling it "psychotherapy" or "psychoanalytic psychotherapy", rather than "psychoanalysis", as I did just above. Within the American Psychoanalytic Association a committee devoted to "psychoanalysis in the community", under the leadership of Stuart Twemlow and Bruce Sklarew (Sklarew, Twemlow, & Wilkinson, 2014), provided a forum for presentation of psychoanalytically oriented or informed clinical work out of the office, in the community (as if there were no community context for the private office). Out-of-office work took place in homeless shelters (Felix, 2014), in schools (Sacramone, 2012) and, in residential treatment centers of various types (as was reported in a British context by Sprince (2002). This work was rarely if ever referred to, straight-up, as "psychoanalysis". A journal in which such out-of-office work was described and theorized was called "The Journal of *Applied* Psychoanalytic Studies" (italics mine) as if in-office work on the couch, multiple times per week, was somehow a platonic form of psychoanalysis, ungrounded in, uncontaminated by, the real world. In traditional case reports in psychoanalytic journals, there was virtually never a mention of a fee, of the process by which it was negotiated, and of the financial or other needs of analyst and analysand, as if to include such negotiations in the case reports would compromise the purity of the analytic procedure. Only in the newly emergent "relational" literature were such issues taken up and discussed (Bass, 2007; Mitchell, 1988; Pizer, 1999), albeit rarely, as inherent aspects of the psychoanalytic process (Figure 0.1).

"He's *still* in therapy."

Figure 0.1 He is still in therapy

I emphasize that my point here is that selectively not paying attention to the community context of psychoanalytic therapy has a limiting effect on the work, *not* that community engagement necessarily has a salutary effect on individual mental health. Very often, individual mental health is promoted by social and community connections. Nonetheless, community connection can reinforce dysfunctional patterns of all sorts in individuals. Loyalty to community can work against individual change that might be otherwise desirable. Social isolation is often pathogenic; social connections can go either way.

1 Community Psychoanalysis Transplanted from Europe to the United States and Beyond

Contemporary psychoanalysis started with Sigmund Freud, even though the roots can be traced much farther back. Similarly, Community Psychoanalysis began with Freud in 1919 when he expressed the well-known wish or expectation that "at some time or other" the "conscience of society" would awaken and

> remind it that the poor man should have just as much right to assistance for his mind as he has now to the life-saving help offered by surgery—such treatments will be free..———. We shall then be faced by the task of adapting our technique to the new conditions. It is very probable too that the large scale application of our therapy will compel us to alloy the pure gold of our therapy freely with the copper of direct suggestion—. it's most effective and most important ingredients will assuredly remain those borrowed from strict and non tendentious psychoanalysis.
>
> (1919, pp. 167–168)

Freud spoke to, and from, the culture of "Red Vienna", a brief flowering of socialism in parts of Europe after World War I.

Several of Freud's points here deserve emphasis. First, there is a lack of urgency in Freud's call for a "psychotherapy for the people". He writes, "some time or other". Nonetheless, the analysts of Europe got right to work; within 13 years all the analytic institutes of Europe had formed free or low-cost clinics. These thrived in the left-wing political environment of the time. This period was brief because within 13 years the Nazis took power (Danto, 2005). By the end of the decade of the 1930s, the European analysts, Jewish for the most part, were driven out of Central Europe to South and Central America, England, and the United States where capitalism and individualism were well entrenched. Some, especially Otto Fenichel and Marie Langer, brought with them their left-wing political commitments. Marie Langer (1989) migrated to Argentina, then to Nicaragua, where she set up a mental health system for the Communist Sandinista government. In Central America, the mental health fields were strongly influenced by the "liberation psychology"

DOI: 10.4324/9781003661146-2

movement organized by the Jesuit priest Ignacio Martin-Baro (1994). He was assassinated in El Salvador in 1989, along with many other Jesuits who had been preaching opposition to the domination of Central American economies by US corporate interests. Throughout the post-World War II period there were active struggles between North American capitalism and socialist resistance. Communitarian psychoanalysis survived when and where there was a strong resistance to US economic domination.

Such was not the case in the United States itself. Otto Fenichel migrated to the United States where he, in the face of the strongly capitalist US economy, tried to organize emigre analysts with socialist leanings. Although Fenichel did not meet the same fate as Martin-Baro, he, along with his socialist colleagues, withdrew from politically inspired commitments (Jacoby, 1983) intimidated by the House Un-American Activities Committee led by Joseph McCarthy. Seeking safety and security in the private sector in the United States, most analysts holed up in their private offices.

Despite Freud's contemptuous reference to the United States as "dollaria" the individualistic and materialistic values of the United States remained dominant and persistently saturated the theory and practice of psychoanalysis. The pathway to prosperity and safety in the United States led through clinical work with affluent patients in private offices, largely moving in the opposite direction from that which Freud tried to stimulate in his 1919 article.

Thus, in the United States in particular, the underlying structure of traditional psychoanalysis, in the form of its individualistic and materialistic values, both reinforced the exclusionary trends in the larger society and distorted the theory and practice of psychoanalysis as applied to mainstream people, socially marginalized people, and the elite as well.

Gambits from Asia Declined: India

A second potential starting point for Community Psychoanalysis was in India in 1923. In one of the first challenges to Freud's control of psychoanalysis Girindrasekhar Bose dared to differ with Freud by claiming that the Oedipus complex, as Freud described it, did not unfold in India the way Freud thought it did. According to Bose, masculinity and femininity were not polarized as they were in Europe, so female identifications did not make Indian men as anxious as it evidently made European men; castration anxiety was deprived of its role as a universal bedrock fact of psychic life. Bose took issue with Freud by claiming that one piece of the puzzle was not the same in India as in Europe. It was never fully agreed between them which pieces of the edifice might remain intact; eventually Freud withdrew from the conversation.

If Freud had been more open minded, he might have learned from Bose's challenge that psychoanalysis would reflect the particular cultural context, or community, in which one or another version of psychoanalysis was situated. But Freud, in part because he didn't want psychoanalysis to be marginalized in *fin-de-siècle* Vienna as a Jewish science, was determined to claim that the theory was universally applicable.

Along similar lines, Afsani Najmabadi (2005) documents that today's signature markers of gender in Iran were reversed only a little more than 100 years ago. In her book *Women with Moustaches and Men without Beards: Gender and Sexual Anxieties of Iranian Modernity* she shows that the idea that beards are a marker of masculinity, smooth facial skin a marker of femininity, was a European import, thus showing the flexibility of gender categories in Iran as in India and presumably elsewhere.

It is noteworthy that the conversation between Freud and Bose, had it been seriously pursued, might have anticipated and accelerated decades of conversation and divisive controversy about gender and the polarization of gender categories, not to mention the place of psychoanalysis in culture. There also could have been an expanded conversation about the Oedipus complex, one that we are only now getting around to addressing.

For such a central part of Freud's theory, the Oedipus complex and associated ideas about gender to which Freud adhered so firmly was a curiously flawed concept. For one thing, while purporting to be a universal theory, it excluded half of humanity: it only applied to males. In order to apply to females, Freud needed to invent penis envy to replace castration anxiety. This theoretical move was clearly a stretch. Did Freud expect us to join him in thinking that the fear of losing "the" penis was the central fact of masculine life, while the envy of males' possession of that organ (even though men were so terrified and preoccupied with losing it) was the cornerstone of the female psyche? Someone like Bose, and many women, might have been expected to come along and ask: is "it" worth all the agita? Freud might have welcomed Bose's intervention. It could have gotten him off the hook, out of the dead end he had gotten himself into. Instead, psychoanalysts spent decades trying, unsuccessfully, to sort all this out, at the cost of many potential adherents.

Psychoanalytic Diaspora

The unitary world of psychoanalysis broke into a number of tributaries as the Nazis came to power in Vienna in the late 1930s scattering the analysts to far-flung parts of the world. Thenceforth, varied schools of psychoanalysis fell under the influence of diverse local cultural communities.

In England, there was an impetus pushing analysts toward making psychoanalysis more accessible to less educationally and economically privileged. With the dismantling of the British Empire in the last seven-plus decades, demographics of the population in England shifted to include residents of the former colonies (some of which are now called the "Commonwealth"): India-Pakistan, Jamaica and other West Indian/Caribbean islands nations, and many others. Prior to the dissolution of the empire, the population of British cities was relatively ethnically homogenous. Due to the history of large-scale slavery in North America, the cities of the United States, post-emancipation, were relatively diverse, containing large numbers of people of African origin. In the United Kingdom, the descendants of slaves were largely scattered in the colonies and former colonies. As decolonization proceeded, the former colonies became autonomous nations. Emigration increased, as did the Caribbean-born and Asia-born population of London and other British cities. With the National Health Service committed to serving *all* the people of England, clinics like Tavistock-Portman, with its psychoanalytic tradition, took on the challenge of serving a diverse, multicultural patient population. In the Jim Crow United States, by contrast, racial segregation was deeply embedded, with psychoanalysis ensconced in the private sector, located in the more affluent neighborhoods where fees were high. With a relatively diverse population, health services and mental health services were, and remain, sharply segregated in the United States.

During and after World War II, the analysts of Europe fled to North and South America and England, each with its own history of slavery and colonialism. The North America economy being so capitalistic, it is not surprising that mental health services were overwhelmingly located in the private sector, in private practice. The public sector survived, relatively better funded when the Democratic Party controlled the levers of power, in the Kennedy-Johnson years, for example. Years of Republican Party domination, particularly the Joseph McCarthy years, was a prime example of how an expanding public sector tended to be demonized, conflated with communism. The psychoanalytic frame fit well within private practice in which there was a premium on privacy, verbal facility, self-sufficiency, a de-emphasis on need gratification. Criteria of analyzability, the ideal "good patient" (Guttman, 1961), was a product of "good" (aka private) schools and highly educated, verbally oriented parents. Psychoanalysis evolved in such a way as to give a higher status to the privileged product (white, affluent) of the North American educational system. Freud, visiting the United States, was skeptical: he referred to the United States as "dollaria". Nonetheless, psychoanalysis was segregated into the economically privileged sectors of US society.

Ultimately, psychoanalysis in the United States became entrenched in office-based private practice, for the most part, a high-priced medical specialty. Thus embedded in mainstream values of its time and place, psychoanalysis remained, with isolated exceptions, located in a fundamentally individualistic orientation as stated (originally) by Freud.

The social location of psychoanalysis among the economically and educationally privileged, however, went against the grain of social justice values that were held by many politically left-leaning US analysts, however ambivalently. So there were psychoanalytic projects, at least on the margins, that aimed to make psychoanalysis more inclusive and accessible.

Twemlow et al. (2014) brought together, in their writing, a number of examples of community-based psychoanalytic projects in the United States. Notable among these was a "healthy community" initiative in Topeka, Kansas

(Twemlow & Wilkinson, 2014). The city government had gotten distracted and paralyzed by a trivial matter (placement of a stop sign) and missed the deadline to apply for a multi-million dollar grant. In another case (Sacco & Twemlow, 1997; Twemlow & Sacco, 1996) there was a Community Psychoanalytic intervention in a Jamaican city with an "extraordinarily high" homicide rate, where the police were routinely referred to as "animals". The interventions in this case included teaching the police nonviolent self-defense to reduce routine police use of guns, and removing bars from police stations, where formerly police had been provided alcohol to reduce their anxiety. In a third case (Bragin, 2005), former child soldiers in Angola were assigned to keep the peace on roads transporting peace-keepers, thus putting sublimated forms of violence to peaceful use.

In these cases, the identified problem was a community dysfunction (violence in Jamaica and Angola, self-defeating behavior in Topeka) that could be remedied once various individuals and groups were persuaded to work together to identify the sources, triggers, and potential solutions to a shared problem. These case reports, however, leave out the process by which someone representing the community asked for help in analyzing and solving the problem, and the negotiations over how this was to be accomplished. Alliance formation is at least half the job of community-based practitioners.

The diagnosis and therapeutics of community dysfunction draws on defense mechanisms with origins in individual psychoanalysis: Topeka as a community was weakened by internal splits that could be remedied by "therapists" who communicated with everyone. In Jamaica, the community was strengthened by the recognition that police had recourse to counterproductive defenses: alcohol and violence. In Angola, Freud's concept of sublimation was brilliantly useful. Those who intervened were successful because their therapeutic efforts were addressed to the community as a whole. We would know more if the authors had told us more about how they were enlisted and how they navigated through and around obstacles within the community. What "resistance" did they encounter and how did they address it? In another report, Twemlow and Wilkinson (2014) reveal that the team in Topeka steered clear of the capitalist (business) community in Topeka, perhaps reflecting their communitarian bias, which, in the end, limited the effectiveness of their work. It pays to keep an eye on countertransference, which operates on the group level, as well as on the individual level, as revealed in Community Psychoanalysis.

In the United States, community-oriented projects found a home within the American Psychoanalytic Association. A committee devoted to "psychoanalysis in the community", under the leadership of Stuart Twemlow and Bruce Sklarew (Sklarew et al., 2004), provided a forum for presentation of psychoanalytically oriented or informed clinical work out of the office, in the community, as noted above.

2 Extended Diaspora

Sigmund Freud, with most of his retinue, and Anna Freud were finally convinced to flee Vienna and the Nazis. They resettled in London, joining Melanie Klein who, invited by Freud biographer, Ernest Jones, had already moved there in 1926. In 1920 Freud (1920) had proposed a second drive, a death instinct, or Thanatos. The dual instinct theory, encompassing life and death instincts, was the foundation for Klein's theoretical advances, most importantly, the theory of positions, paranoid-schizoid and depressive, as an alternative to Anna Freud's (1966) ego psychology with its stage-based theory highlighting ego development. In 1946, Klein (1952) introduced the concept of "projective identification" which, by positing that the defense of projection entails a recipient, as well as a projector, opened a new link between the intrapsychic and social/interpersonal/external world.

There were other factors in England conducive to encouraging emergence and development of more flexible and accessible versions of psychoanalytic treatment, despite the relative rigidity of Kleinian technique. In England, the bifurcation between private and public sectors was less polarized, as the Tavistock institute, a major center of psychoanalytic training and practice, especially with children and adolescents, became part of the British National Health Service. In the post-war United States something similar occurred as the Community Mental Health movement, with some government funding, drew some psychoanalytically inclined clinicians into the public sector (Altman, 1995, 2010; Pine, 1985). With time, psychoanalytically oriented therapists in private as well as public settings began to adapt to the increasingly culturally diverse patients knocking on the door expecting to find services mandated by the Community Mental Health Act. US analysts gradually practiced with more technical freedom but were often careful to limit the scope of what they were doing by calling it "psychotherapy" or "psychoanalytic psychotherapy", rather than "psychoanalysis".

The economies of England and other countries in Europe, less wary of socialism/communism than the United States, adopted National Health services, accessible to all, with less turmoil than could have occurred in the United States. Psychoanalysis was integrated into the National Health Service, in places like the Tavistock and Portman clinic (TPC), where, increasingly,

DOI: 10.4324/9781003661146-3

it encountered a multicultural, socioeconomically diverse group of patients. Faced with large immigrant populations struggling with complex tasks of adapting to a new culture, language, discrimination in employment and housing, limited financial resources, and a history of colonial oppression, TPC adopted new treatment models which stretched the traditional psychoanalytic frame. With the concept of projective identification in place, the stage was set for the application of psychoanalysis across cultural and socioeconomic boundaries. In the United States where the dominant theory was the stage-based ego psychology with its maturity ethic, such an application of psychoanalysis entailed a hierarchy. Interacting with racial and economic hierarchies in the United States, the result was a hierarchical psychoanalysis: pure gold for the elite, alloys for the masses.

Hierarchies, especially ego-based hierarchies, also conduce to childism (Young-Bruehl, 2012), the denigration of children. Childism interacting with sexism conduced to the undervaluation of people who work with children, especially in the United States. In England, the authors of innovation in psychoanalysis were people with honored places in the field, who nonetheless worked with children (Anna Freud, Melanie Klein, D.W. Winnicott, who put mothers high up in his pantheon, in contrast to Freud who sometimes marginalized mothers, or worse).

Child psychotherapy at the Tavistock clinic was already relatively flexible, given the inevitable involvement of families, often extended families, schools, and other outside agencies. Work with family and social welfare systems had precedents at TPC; The Tavistock Center, already a center of innovation in group therapy and organizational consultation, often informed by psychoanalytic theory (Bion, 1987, 1988), gave rise to systemic interventions in residential treatment centers. The *Journal of Child Psychotherapy* provided a forum for presentations of systemic interventions, guided by a psychoanalytically based emphasis on group-level defense mechanisms (e.g., Menzies-Lyth, 1975; Sprince, 2002). The A. K. Rice Institute blazed this trail in the United States, largely in isolation from the psychoanalytic tradition of analysis of resistance and defense out of which it, nonetheless, emerged. Following Bion (1987) this line of thought articulated the sources of extreme anxiety evoked by group experiences, linking them to group-level defenses. This work was exemplified by Menzies-Lyth (1975) who studied a hospital nursing service, starting with the severe anxieties about illness and death with which nurses are continually confronted. These permeate hospitals and, particularly, the daily work of nurses. They trigger the defenses that structure their work for better and worse. For example, Menzies-Lyth pointed out that nurses split up their duties by task, rather than by patient. The experience is an action, not necessarily a human connection. One nurse measures blood pressure, another empties bed pans. When a patient dies or his condition deteriorates, the nurse's death anxiety, guilt, and sense of loss is modulated. On the other hand, the human attachment that, ultimately, is the source of meaningfulness for a nurse is submerged in a sea of detached mechanized actions.

Fakhry Davids (2010), likewise, regarded racism as a constellation of defensive phenomena, most fundamentally splitting. In a multi-racial context, anxieties around destructiveness and guilt are defended against by dividing people into two groups: those like me, my people, and those unlike me, the others. This is an age-old strategy, an infantile strategy, for keeping good and bad separate. When applied to people of different skin colors or other varying physical characteristics, onto which psychological and behavioral characteristics are mapped, the stage is set for individual and systemic racism; the enemy, threat or badness, is readily identifiable and attacked without guilt. A host of psychological complexities are simplified and resolved, though at the cost of social conflict. Davids believes such conflicts cannot be approached without recognition of the childhood defensive pattern, an intrapsychically installed constellation, originally installed by an outer situation. Once the internal racist constellation gets activated, the internal constellation gets reinforced all around. A vicious circle is initiated; Davids believes therapeutic priority needs to be given to the powerful and pre-existing infantile pattern.

Thomas Main, a British psychologist, conducted a study of nurses and other health professionals in the hospital where he worked. He found a recurring pattern among the staff concerned with the care of patients that he called "special". These were patients who were described by referring sources as having a great deal of positive potential, but having been allegedly poorly served by previous treatments. On admission, these patients typically made demands for special treatment, special privileges, not accorded to ordinary patients. If, as typically happened, one professional gave in to such demands, the staff quickly formed two groups: one, a one-person "in group" typically the psychotherapist, who perceived themselves and were perceived by the "special" patient, as uniquely attuned to that person's special, but unrealistic, needs. The second group (everyone else) was perceived as insensitive and hostile. Once this pattern was established, it never ended well. The pattern became self-reinforcing, as one of the special privileges accorded to the patient was to have an ally, one person, who deeply understood how poorly treated the patient felt by the rest of the world. The rest of the world, i.e. the remainder of the staff, of course, resented being thus characterized. For an observer entering a ward split up in this way, it would seem obvious that a dysfunctional system was having a pathogenic effect on the "special" patient. Main thought the special patient had a way of initiating this development by inducing or seducing one staff member to provide special privileges. Main's conclusion, or prescription, for avoiding this pathogenic development consisted of advice for hospital staff as follows:

If at any time you are impelled to instruct others to be less hostile and more loving than they can truly be—don't!

(Main, 1957/1989, p. 145)

Main (1989) believed that the pattern he described derived from the primitive anxieties evoked when hospital staff found themselves unable to help suffering patients. Following Klein (1952) Main posited that to ward off this anxiety, the staff, as a group, split off one person as a successful healer, while the rest of the staff had to bear the burden of inability to make reparation for their internalized destructiveness. Gabbard (1986) and Stanton and Schwartz (1954) found similar patterns in other hospitals. Along with Menzies, these researchers found links between intrapsychic dynamics and defenses, and dysfunctional group dynamics. There could not be a more clear illustration of the problems generated by splitting.

Sprince (2002) also made meaning of group dynamics and countertransference among staff in a residential treatment center for traumatized children and adolescents in England. She was guided by Kleinian and Bionian theory, utilizing concepts of projective identification:

> I was frequently terrified. I recognized pretty quickly that the teachers and care staff were organizing referrals that would ensure that I would get to have the frightening and overwhelming experiences that they endured—they were setting me a test: if I could survive and still come out able to think about the childrens' feelings, they would begin to trust my way of working.
>
> (p. 147)

Sprince further describes how she imagined the children's mental states:

> Their minds are like minefields: at any moment something may trigger a memory of terrible pain and humiliation. So they retreat into a mindless, unthinking way of getting through the day. When a painful feeling threatens to erupt, they look for any way of escaping from it: this can be through sex, violence, drugs, drink, or a myriad other forms of delinquency.
>
> (p. 148)

Unmanageable behavior here gets understood, in a way that brings together psychoanalytic and systemic modes of thinking, as a way of managing psychic trauma and pain. Psychoanalytic thinking provides a containing structure for the therapists' minds to help them cope with the residents' destructive behavior.

Sprince tries to help the staff with their countertransference feelings: Again, quoting Sprince:

> One young man described how he felt he had to put on armor against the childrens' feelings whenever he came to work. We discussed how this related to the childrens' need to numb themselves against horrific experiences of parental abuse.
>
> (p. 152)

Sexual affairs among the staff were talked about and thought about in the context of the sexually charged atmosphere among these sexually abused adolescents as well as in instances of abuse in the staffs' own personal histories.

In the end, the increasing socioeconomic and cultural diversity among patients in both the United Kingdom and the United States, interacting with Kleinian theoretical models in the United Kingdom, and with ego/psychological theoretical models in the United States, led to divergent outcomes. Perhaps the important factor, already noted, was that Kleinian theory was position-based, applying to everyone, while ego psychology was stage based, lending itself to a split between mature—healthy therapists—and immature—sick—patients. When technique was adapted, it was often seen as an adaptation to the limitation of the patient, rather than a purposeful overriding of the therapist's refusal to admit to their own limitations, their own anxieties and defenses. Kleinian theory, in the end, was a very useful splitting work-around.

Psychoanalytic thinking in the United Kingdom more readily became a containing structure in the minds of the consultant and the staff. Acting out that reproduces trauma could thus be replaced with thought, ultimately with grief. Prison inmates, with whom Kita (2019) worked, described this process as "flipping the narrative". Emmanuel (1996) and Kliman (2011) employed similar forms of narrative flipping to understand difficulties foster children had in forming stable attachments to caregivers.

Harlem Family Institute

At this point it is important to note the Harlem Family Institute (HFI) which for decades had trained clinicians in New York to practice psychoanalytic therapy outside an office setting. HFI for over 30 years had described itself as a psychoanalytic institute but outside the structures of the American Psychoanalytic Association (APSA) and the International Psychoanalytic Association (IPA). HFI was based in Harlem, a community historically known for its predominantly African-American population. Since the 1960s, East Harlem has seen an influx of Latinx residents, and beginning in the 2000s, Central and West Harlem have attracted White residents as rental prices increased throughout New York City. Among the founders of HFI was Margaret Morgan Lawrence, the first African-American psychoanalyst; Harvard psychiatrist Robert Coles, the author of *Children of Crisis: A Study of Courage and Fear* (1967), *The Political Life of Children* (2007), and a number of other books; and Steven Kurtz (1977), a psychoanalyst who started HFI at the "storefront", an independent tuition-free school in Harlem. For years HFI existed outside of, or at the margins of the institutional psychoanalytic world, training clinicians to work with overlapping marginalized people: children, the children of Harlem.

Harlem Family Services

HFI portrayed itself as a psychoanalytic institute, unique in its focus on Harlem with its African-American population and its alliances with schools as community-based venues for the clinical training of its candidates. HFI was not a multi-service mental health center for the Harlem community, which was grossly underserved. HFI did not participate in the Community Mental Health movement of the 1960s and did not apply for funding as a Community Mental Health Center. There was no affiliation with nearby psychoanalytic institutes, though Lawrence had trained in the neighborhood at the Columbia University Center for Psychoanalytic Training and Research, which trained candidates to work with multiple age groups in private offices.

All this changed in the 2010s in connection with HFI's connection with the APSA initiative, to be discussed below, to promote the development in its institutes of training tracks in Community Psychoanalysis. Some of those involved in that initiative, including Neil Altman, Paula Kliger, Gilbert Kliman, Sheila Johnson, and Michael Conolly, who for over a decade had been the Director of HFI, took steps to spin off a full-service mental health clinic for Harlem called "Harlem Family Services", with full approval from New York State. In many ways the APSA initiative was and is the next stage in the US Community Mental Health movement. As of this writing, state approval is pending; early indications are positive. A forensic psychiatry project is already underway, led by Gilbert Kliman, called the "Social Justice Division" of Harlem Family Services, under the auspices of which forensic psychiatric reports were produced for the use of law firms representing people claiming damages from Child Welfare Agencies and other entities that allegedly failed in their duty to protect children from abuse and/or neglect. Fees from the production of these reports are available for HFS's "start-up" expenses while HFS awaits state approval to offer clinical services. Once state approval is granted, HFS will be able to bill Medicaid and other health insurance providers for clinical services and apply for grants (tax exempt status is already in place for donations to HFS as a registered charity). Thus, the mental health resources available to the residents of Harlem will finally begin to catch up to what is ordinarily available to residents in New York City's more privileged communities.

3 Community Psychoanalysis Takes Many Forms

Therapeutic Communities

Therapeutic communities exist in many places around the world. Some are half-way houses, day treatment or partial hospitalization programs, intended to support people as part of the process of discharge from psychiatric hospitalization or from residential detoxification or drug treatment programs. Some people are deemed to need a high level of psychosocial support but do not qualify for inpatient treatment. Partial hospitalization programs were required parts of Community Mental Health Centers funded by governmental agencies in the United States at a time when governments were trying to save money with less restrictive, and costly, treatments for people with severe mental disorders. These also include undomiciled or insecurely domiciled adolescents. Corresponding facilities are "residential treatment programs", which may include schools, vocational counseling, and assistance finding housing.

See the case study of Sprince (2002), a typical example of psychoanalytic clinical group therapy conducted in a residential facility.

Gilbert Kliman and Reflective Network Therapy

Gilbert Kliman is a child analyst who developed a way of working with preschool age children that he called "reflective network therapy" (RNT). RNT emphasizes many of the key elements often missing in traditional psychoanalytic projects. These run the gamut from empirical outcome research to engagement with the community, the network, of concerned and involved people around the identified patient.

The networks in question are preschools for young children on the autistic spectrum as well as traumatized preschool children who have poorly developed reflective function, i.e. the capacity or inclination to self-reflect, to mentalize (Fonagy et al., 2002). Psychotherapy with such children aims to enhance mentalization and self-reflectiveness (Alvarez, 1992). Teachers and other staff in RNT classrooms are trained and oriented to facilitate discussions of the mental states, the intentions and feelings, underlying behavior. These discussions take place in the classroom's public space and may

DOI: 10.4324/9781003661146-4

involve anyone and everyone within earshot. As these conversations unfold, the classroom becomes a reflective network, usable for therapeutic purposes for the benefit of the individuals therein and for the benefit of the group itself.

In the deceptively simple name of this technique, Kliman captured the very essence of Community Psychoanalysis. "Reflectiveness" is a mental quality, a quintessentially human activity. Here it is seen as a quality of a "network", more like a community than a person. Kliman's approach aims to generate a network/community characterized by reflectiveness.

Kliman thereby cuts through the boundaries that theretofore artificially separated psychoanalysis from other clinical and research activities, thus potentially enriching all around. In the clinical realm, Kliman's technique enabled parents and teachers to contribute observations, thoughts, and questions about children's feelings, to initiate discussions that might otherwise be deprived of important perspectives. Since the objects of discussion were typically events that were open to observation by everyone, areas that were restricted by confidentiality considerations were much restricted.

Kliman made important advances documenting outcomes of RNT. Documentation of positive outcomes from psychoanalytic treatment is frequently stymied by unproductive controversies about what constitutes bona fide psychoanalysis. More problematically, there is a history of psychoanalysis regarding itself, and being regarded, as self-justifying, so that acceptance by the patient of the analyst's interpretations is seen as evidence in itself, of progress or improvement. Ultimately, in the public mind, "fixing the game" in this way often leads to skepticism, if not cynicism, about psychoanalysis.

Kliman has given a high priority to empirical documentation of improvement in the lives of children and families. RNT in public spaces enables ratings based on data collected from multiple observers, teachers, and other adults and children in the classroom. Kliman (unpublished) developed behavior-based and observable criteria for rating the presence or absence of an analytic process, e.g. as an example of "preparatory phenomena", Kliman (unpublished) includes: "Analyst's observation of child's interpersonal action, when shared with the child, leads the child to talk with the analyst about his inner life more than earlier in the session, or leads to more sublimated action". In the category of "criteria of deepening analysis" Kliman included, for example, "Work on a dream leads to a day residue or expression of a wish, memory or an affect not apparent earlier in the treatment, or leads to shared scrutiny of defenses or shared scrutiny of transference material". Under "Criteria of well-established" analysis: Kliman includes, for example, "interpretation of reaction formation leads to some expression of defended against impulse in derivative or undisguised form". One could try to refine such criteria, but in any case, raters and ratings could be held to accepted standards of validity and reliability.

His assessment of treatment outcomes similarly relied on criteria held to generally accepted standards of validity and reliability. Measures such as increases of IQ scores touch on both process and outcome (Kliman, 2011).

Kliman expanded his conception of outcome to include indirect ways in which his interventions enhanced the lives of his patients, their families, and their communities. For example, Kliman engaged the damage done by childhood sexual abuse immediately as well as many years after the fact. His court testimony in connection with lawsuits against governmental child protective agencies, sometimes many years later, resulted in monetary settlements of hundreds of thousands of dollars. While money cannot undo the damage caused by childhood abuse, acknowledgment of damage by the community can reassure the grown-up victim that his or her suffering is real and acknowledged by society.

Additionally, Kliman and his collaborators have given a high priority to development of materials, such as explanatory workbooks that have face validity in helping young children cope with trauma and stress. Starting with questionnaires and then guided activity workbooks on topics related to the assassination of president Kennedy (Wolfenstein and Kliman, G. 1965) natural disasters, war, earthquakes, and floods, Kliman and his group have provided materials to help children acknowledge and address pain and suffering in the world at large. His group has done an enormous amount to encourage active engagement and citizenship among children. He believes that "childism", i.e., prejudice against children, is manifest in a variety of forms of neglect of the welfare of children, in war zones, under conditions of economic poverty.

Kliman's efforts in this regard undermine the widespread idea that adults cannot talk with children about the difficult, even horrifying, realities of life. The belief that it is the responsibility of adults to shield children from pain because they are too young, too immature, to process such realities is of a piece with the belief, to which Kliman objected, that young children do not possess the mental and emotional apparatus to suffer depression and to grieve. A difference of opinion on this point, early in his career, with Martha Wolfenstein (at the Albert Einstein College of Medicine), was at least part of what led him to find a more receptive audience for his counter-childist belief that children can indeed grieve, that, in fact, they need help doing so. Adults need to give some thought to *how* to talk with children about painful realities, about which Kliman knew a great deal already from personal experience as a child, having endured multiple bouts of potentially fatal illnesses, surgeries, being left alone frequently and for long periods as a preschooler, being awakened by his father's screams at night amidst nightmare flashbacks from World War II and more.

Anna Freud (1989) discouraged psychoanalytic thinking about childhood depression and treatment of child or adult analysands during grieving processes by highlighting how the immaturity of the childhood psyche made grieving and depression, as seen in adults, seem inconceivable. She thought children, unable to wrap their minds around the permanence and irreversibility of death, would not realize that a loved person was gone forever. Sigmund Freud's theory, according to which the superego developed only upon gradual resolution of the Oedipus complex in middle childhood, seemed to imply that the self-punitive action of the superego could only be a later development. Thus, Anna Freud and her followers suggested that depression, involving as it does the superego in a self-punitive way, could not manifest, at least as it does in adults.

Melanie Klein (1952), meanwhile, was putting superego development into a fundamentally different theoretical context. With her primary focus on destructiveness derived from the death instinct, she thought an early form of the superego, saturated with destructive and aggressive energy (though in a tiny body), was present from early infancy. This unmodulated destructiveness, in what Klein called the "paranoid-schizoid position", gave rise to the "depressive position" in which love and destructive energy, constructive and destructive energy, existed side by side, modulating each other. In short, Klein's contribution made it possible to think about superego development as occurring earlier, ideally more gradually, than it appeared in Freudian theories.

In this context of theoretical evolution, Kliman was able to contemplate how very young, and developmentally delayed, children could be helped to cope with destructive forces in the world around them and in themselves. As a child in the wake of World War II and the Jewish Holocaust and in the Brooklyn streets of his neighborhood, Kliman was surrounded by the bullies of childhood, and at home, by unmistakably grieving and depressed adults. He became finely attuned to their emotional states, beginning to wonder if and how he could help. Thus were sown the seeds which were to sprout, much later, into his therapeutic innovations.

We can't pin down what allowed child-Gilbert to discover inner resources that made it possible for him to make lemonade out of the lemons of trauma and post-traumatic suffering surrounding him. We can note, however, that he suffered considerably from being left alone, that the suffering of his parents and other family members offered itself as an obvious way to connect by trying to make them happy with his accomplishments, since his parents made it clear that they were appreciative of their son's verbal intelligence and intellectual achievement.

There are extensive reviews of psychoanalytically oriented clinical work and school-based programs in Sarason, Levine, Goldenberg, Cherlin, and Bennett (Sarason et al., 1966), Music and Hall (2008), Sacramone (2012), and Altman (2015, pp. 79–84). The marginal status in the institutional psychoanalytic world of the Harlem Family Institute (see pp. 13 above), along with the paucity of Child Clinical Psychology training programs, testifies to the prevalence of childism, i.e. prejudice against children (Kliman, 2011; Young-Bruehl, 2012) in the field (see pp. cxxx above). Psychological work with children is largely taught in School Psychology training programs, split off from Clinical Psychology programs. Community Psychology is likewise split off from Clinical Psychology. Community-based clinical work is taught in Social Work programs, split off from Psychology graduate programs, to the detriment of the latter. When school-based work is discussed, its practitioners are commonly described as in need of consciousness-raising by psychoanalysts. Malberg (2008) wrote of:

> --------adapting and translating our psychoanalytic language in order to develop a common framework between the different systems influencing the life of the young person. It was our refusal to be excluded from the school and family systems and their politics that helped us to reflect on, and understand the behavior of some of these young people as a developmental adaptation to a failure of their environment to understand their emotional needs.
>
> (p. 102)

What about the other way around?

Schools Part 2: Teaching and Learning During the COVID Emergency

> Children have never been very good at listening to their elders, but they have never failed to imitate them.
>
> James Baldwin (1962)

Kindness, Violence, and Hypocrisy in Schools

In recent years I have noticed an increased emphasis on "kindness" in the education of children and adolescents. At the same time, bullying, mass shootings, and other forms of violence are much in the public eye. There are recurrent calls for gun control, perennially failing to make progress against unyielding resistance. Gun violence pervades the media, for the most part uncountered by warnings to parents. How to reconcile the split in the way we socialize children, between the focus on kindness in teaching and preaching and the reality of violence in the streets and in the media which we tolerate and support? We should be thinking deeply about the conflicting messages being transmitted to our young people and the potential for our teachings to be dismissed by them as hypocritical, something adolescents, in particular, are prone to do anyway. Do we reflect on the experience of children and adolescents being exposed to adults in leadership positions advocating violence on television, on the internet, and on the newsstands they pass on their way to school? Do we reflect on the possibility that if young people do not conclude that adults are hypocritical, we are training them to deal with contradiction and complexity by ignoring some of the evidence of their senses? Baldwin was likely warning the adult world that we are training succeeding generations, not only in hypocrisy but in dissociation and cynicism.

Meanwhile, during the early phases of the COVID pandemic, children and adolescents witnessed their elders passionately debating, arguing, about masks, vaccinations, and opening and closing schools and businesses like stores. Some adults claimed that such measures were essential for containing the virus that had sickened and killed millions of people, while other adults claimed, equally passionately, that such measures made matters worse, causing the illness, the financial and emotional devastation of unemployment and insecure employment that many could witness in their own homes and families. Schools closed, leaving bewildered children and frazzled parents stranded with each other.

My impression is that as this situation unfolded, parents, children, teachers, and the administrators responsible for public policy were, for the most part, overwhelmed, lurching from crisis to crisis, struggling to keep their heads above water. Some influential people in public life consistently invoked the authority of science, while biotech companies resolutely worked on vaccines in the face of anti-vaxxers.

Long before the COVID pandemic, inconsistency between professed values and the reality of public and private life was pervasive in the United States. Consider the long-standing contradictions around race and social class. Adults, some of them anyway (until the recent abrupt banning of commitments to diversity, equity, and inclusion by the federal government in the United States), professed adherence to the value of diversity and inclusiveness. Yet most children didn't and don't have to look too far to see segregation, uniformity, and injustice. Their schools are mostly composed of children and adults with dark skin or light skin. The people who run the school are likely to have light skin; the maintenance staff, most likely, have dark skin. In upscale restaurants the servers will be light skinned, the runners (who bring the food) will be dark skinned.

All the while there are people who live up to, and beyond, professed values, mostly quietly, without self-aggrandizement, without media attention.

While the pandemic was wreaking havoc, gender categories were being reconsidered and redefined. Public attitudes about sexual orientation, too, were up in the air for many people, with sharp splits along generational lines. Racialized violence intensified. Police murders of Black people and anti-immigrant violence gave rise to "Black Lives Matter" and other movements, and resistance manifest in opposition to "Critical Race Theory" and book banning in schools and libraries. Political, generational, and geographical fault lines deepened as the political landscape underwent tectonic shifts. Politicians discovered that there was electoral advantage in deepening the various divides, generally undermining public confidence in the political process.

How unprecedented is this pervasive and chaotic divisiveness? Is the situation more extreme in quality and extremity from what prevailed in the World Wars, in the Great Depression, in the local wars that are continually breaking out? Is this pandemic fundamentally different from the recurrent pandemics and epidemics that plague our world?

What can be said about how the situation today affects families, children, and adolescents, across age groups, across socio-economic groups, across ethnic and national groups, and across racial lines?

Are there psychologically tenable and developmentally viable ways to help children and adolescents to cope with all this turmoil and confusion?

Talking with Children and Adolescents

I wouldn't say that I quite imitated my parents, as Baldwin said, though I often found, and find, myself being or behaving like them, usually to my dismay. I think my parents shaped me more through my efforts to be Unlike them. But, as we know from psychoanalysis, the irony is that we often affirm through negation.

In the following anecdotes I note how attentively I followed my parents' behavior and how much I inferred about them from what I unconsciously selected to notice. From this, I conclude that we know more than we think we know, an idea reflected in Bollas's idea of the "unthought known" and Donnel Stern's (1997) notion of "unformulated experience". I find something of this sort when I scan my childhood memories: my 5'5" father, for example, looking up at the 6'3" + president of the local bank and flamboyantly telling a story. My father seemed to me to be substituting drama for height. Years later, I put the pieces together: this was Minnesota, this was the president of the bank for non-Jews, my father was a short dark Jew, the president was a tall blond, non-Jew, and it would've been a feather in my father's cap to get this bank's business. These pieces formed a meaningful constellation when I began to think about, to understand, race and ethnicity and social class, where I and my family fit into the mosaic in which I grew up and lived, as well as my father's psychology, his ambitions, his vulnerability. There was a proto-psychologist emerging in my selective attention as well as a proto-social theorist.

Can education systems facilitate the kind of learning that will help our young people to navigate this world we are all thrown into? Children and adolescents in general do not have the cognitive tools or the breadth of experience to put all the pieces together, yet, theoretically, adults, teachers, and parents can jump-start the process by raising questions with children and adolescents in bits and pieces. Questions such as "what does it mean that there are two major banks in St Paul, and why is the president of one tall and blond, while the president of the other is short and dark like my father?" Why do most of the Jews live on one side of town, whereas Black people live on "another side of" town?

I suggest that Bollas's concept of "unthought known" and Stern's of "unformulated experience" can alert us to a continuum of knowing, of formulation, and of consciousness. We can add here Freud's (1900) notion of the "preconcious", somewhere between unconscious and conscious. With the prefix "pre", Freud seems to imply that in human development, experience tends to move toward consciousness, though there are various forces that can obstruct this movement, and others, such as those contained in psychoanalysis and some forms of literature, that can move things along. The process of education can move things along too. I will have more to say about that shortly.

With this idea of gradations in consciousness, along with the idea that there is an inherent push in the direction of increased levels of consciousness, subject to interference, we can come to an understanding of what it means to think that people can know more than they think they know or can formulate or think consciously. In an early stage of formulation, a little pushback can elicit thoughts like: "I always kind of knew that".

It is this kind of thinking that led me to think that educators and therapists can facilitate development by raising questions like: "why do servers in restaurants tend to be white, while runners tend to be black?"

One major, almost insuperable, obstacle to such conversations is that they are taboo among adults. Adults tend not to talk among themselves about such matters, much less with their children. Children learn what is not to be talked about, what is taboo, by osmosis. This is the process Harry Stack Sullivan (1953) referred to in terms of the contagion of anxiety. Hypocrisy arises from not talking, or even thinking, about the social hierarchies that so fundamentally organize our lives. So one of the pieces that need to be put into place to educate children about the conditions of their lives concerns anxiety, shame, and guilt. Everyone lives these feelings all the time; very rarely does anyone talk about them or admit to them. Yet the taboos are clear to all. Raising such questions, especially with children, activates and challenges these taboos and gets right to the heart of what psychoanalysis is all about.

By adolescence or young adulthood, sometimes it can take only a little push to make some of these pieces fall into place. When my younger daughter was 12, I undertook a little personal research project asking her and others of her age when they first became aware of their racial and ethnic identity. My daughter attended an expensive private school, where, despite professed egalitarian and anti-racist values, a large majority of the students and families were white and upper middle to upper class.

My daughter said that she and her classmates did not make distinctions of race and social class. Everyone was the same in her school.

A few days earlier she had had a "play date" with an African-American friend who lived on the other side of Harlem. (The school they both attended was on the side of Harlem nearer to us, but several blocks into an upper-middle-class neighborhood. Her friend lived in Central Harlem.)

I said:

> But wait a minute, you and I both know where Keisha lives and what it's like over there. How do you think it is for her to travel the five miles everyday from her neighborhood where everyone is black to school in this neighborhood where most everyone is white?

(it didn't occur to me to ask my daughter what it was like for her to visit Keisha a few miles, but worlds away, in Harlem).

My daughter's eyes widened and she said "I never *thought* about that before!" Clearly a thousand pieces of her experience that had been present but not connected explicitly in her mind suddenly came together like magnetic pieces that all crossed an invisible boundary and crashed into each other, forming a new pattern. More than 30 years later, we both still vividly remember that moment.

To go back to my original question: how do we adults go about educating children so that they will recognize and think about social realities hiding in plain sight? How do we deal with the shame and guilt that lurks in a situation in which hugely consequential differences among people coexist with an egalitarian ethic? How do we deal with children and adolescents who, new to this world of high-minded ideals coexisting with prejudice and violence, see the evidence of realities that cannot be spoken?

Many years ago, Isaiah Berlin (1969) noted that we tend to hold diverse values that are incommensurate with each other. Liberty and equality are one example. In a capitalist system I expect to be free to start my own business and to enjoy the profits. I will also deplore the resulting economic and social inequality that follows. I may deny or dissociate evidence of this inequality as I ignore the homeless on the street or rationalize their obvious suffering as due to personal failure, addiction, etc. I will defend to the death, your death that is, my right to the fruits of your labor.

At the same time, I may donate to charities that some have created to alleviate this suffering. I may vote for politicians who advocate for taxation of the monied rich and care for the economically poor, along with acquisition of the tools of violence and world destruction.

Children and adolescents may notice some of these contradictory realities while lacking the capacity to think in complex, multi-faceted ways about the human condition. If we adults, the educators of the young, attempt to cultivate tools to do so, we may be accused of politicizing the schools.

Helping Children and Adolescents to Think about the Unthinkable, in Reality and in Fantasy/Play

In the face of such contradictory realities we adults should be supporting our children in noticing what they see and thinking about what it all means as best they can. On an immediate and concrete level, conflict and violence in the classroom can be the occasion for discussion of feelings of competition, hatred and anger. Such discussions can serve an educational function while, insofar as all children take part, countering the isolation and demonization of those individuals who had acted in a dysregulated manner. On a relatively abstract level, all children should receive some orientation to emotions such as anxiety and fear, guilt and shame. Children at all ages can be encouraged in groups, with the guidance of educators, to identify such feelings in age-appropriate ways, to think of occasions in the classroom and out of the classroom when they felt such emotions, and to think together about the various useful and counterproductive ways people handle such feelings. Is it possible and useful to try to forget or otherwise erase troublesome feelings?

What makes us sad? How can feelings be shared? What makes us angry? What are the advantages and disadvantages of aggressive expression of anger? What are alternatives, their advantages and disadvantages?

Violence in the community, crime, international conflict, and war should be acknowledged and discussed. Even when no solutions are at hand, such as is the case with considerations about school shootings and acts of war in Ukraine, feelings, including rage and helplessness, can be acknowledged and shared. In such cases, literary fiction may be a useful jumping-off point for discussion of unthinkable realities. One among such examples would be Toni Morrison's novel *Beloved* (1987) which concerns a mother who killed her baby rather than allow her to mature into slavery. It is the task of a writer of fiction to transform unbearable realities into representations that do not encourage the reader to look away, while providing a certain distance that makes it bearable to read and to think about the nearly unthinkable. Morrison prepared herself to write *Beloved* by reading slave narratives, the true accounts of life under slavery, and the realities that made a living mother feel it preferable to kill her baby rather than allow her to be a slave.

For older children and young adults there must be a place for them to read such as Isaiah Berlin and James Baldwin, to think about thinking, and to grapple with destructiveness and hatred all around, coexisting with love and constructive work to be done.

I am of the generation of analysts who trained in the incubator of the relational turn, resting on the idea that intrapsychic or mental life, people's thoughts and feelings, could not be understood outside the context of other people. From that point of view, the analyst's effort to observe the patient's mind at work from outside the analytic field, by sitting behind the patient, saying little or nothing except interpretations, and so on, was fundamentally misguided. You can try to be objective like a good scientist, but you can't deny that sitting silently behind the patient has an impact. Harry Stack Sullivan (1953) made this point clearly and economically: the analyst (he said "psychiatrist") is a "participant-observer". An observer, yes, but always also a participant, if only by virtue of his or her effort to disappear.

Winnicott didn't bother trying to conceive of the children outside the influence-field of others. He wrote (Winnicott, 1971): "there is no baby without a mother", and freely contributed his own squiggles in his signature squiggle game.

Play

Winnicott saw psychotherapy and psychoanalysis as occurring in play space, aka transitional space, where fantasy and reality meet. Play, for Winnicott, was serious business, involving unconscious processing of experience. Thomas Ogden (2001) elaborated on Winnicott's point when he wrote that dreaming is always occurring but like the stars is only visible at night when one is not blinded by too much ambient light. Freud was reaching for some similar level of consciousness with his concept of free association or primary process. When he asked his patient to say "whatever comes to mind" he was hoping to bring to the surface the level of dreaming or, perhaps, of poetry. In psychoanalysis there is a level of unconscious communication that may be accessible through bodily experience or marginal thoughts. These Freud was trying to bring to the center, via free association or dream thoughts. Hans Loewald's (1988) contribution was to point to integration of primary process, or dreaming, with secondary process, what we ordinarily call conventional logical thought, as the goal of psychoanalysis. The word "trauma" refers to experience that is inaccessible to unconscious processing, violence, in counterposition to violent fantasy. War, counterposed to war games with GI Joes. In Bion's (1988) language, "beta elements" refers to unsymbolized experience. Beta elements come at you like bullets; we must remember that Bion was a tank commander in World War I. In his language, "Alpha function" transforms beta elements into thinkable, i.e. dreamable, experience.

Clinical work with children provides ready access to play space. Play is the mother tongue of childhood, the way children think and communicate. One day years ago I had a session with a five-year-old girl whose father had lost control and kicked her the day before. She was playing, making a huge mess, refusing to clean up as the end of the session approached and the next patient arrived. I was getting frustrated and impatient; all at once she fell to the floor, lay on her back; I felt like kicking her. As I looked down on her, I said: "you probably think I want to kick you". I don't remember whether I said: "like your father did yesterday". I had to *want* to kick her, and she unconsciously made sure I did. I had to be willing to *feel like* kicking her. I had to let the situation escalate just so much, neither more nor less, so that I would feel enraged and anxious, but without too much anxiety about losing control of myself. My words and the way I spoke them had to convey that I knew what her father felt, but that I would not act. Thus, alpha function transformed a beta element, an act of violence, into a thought. This sequence illustrates my understanding of what Bion meant by containing, including the role of transference and countertransference. I was and wasn't her father, it was reality and fantasy.

Depressive Position

Melanie Klein's (1975) concept of the depressive position in tandem with Winnicott's emphasis on play has opened up psychoanalysis in productive new directions. Klein's concept first depolarized good and bad, transforming a polarity into a dialectic. Subsequent theory has applied the dialectical perspective more broadly to rethink reality and fantasy, work and play, even paranoid-schizoid and depressive positions themselves. Dialectical thinking, or rather dialectical living, coheres with coexistence and non-violence. Polarized thinking coheres with either/or, exclusionary living, violence and murder may follow. But there is no utopia in view, here; both/and applies at every level. If we have access to both dialectical and polarized ways of being, each modifies and moderates the other, as Klein showed how good and bad, love and hate, moderate each other.

We find ourselves living in an increasingly polarized world. In the current context, we have a one-sided emphasis on kindness and zero tolerance for destructiveness, leading, ironically, to harsh punishment and cancel culture. Then we have spikes in mass murder and suicide. The situation cries out for coexistence, non-violence, and tolerance for complexity.

Progressive Education and Psychoanalytic Therapy

Around 1348, Giovanni Boccaccio (1348/2007) wrote *The Decameron*, a series of 100 stories told by young people sitting around a fire in the midst of the plague, the Black Death, near Florence, Italy. Without going into detail, a study of these stories potentially provides the basis for historical study as well as discussion of how literature and other arts and humanities help people process traumatic events like the plague. We can also study how society at that time could not tolerate the Decameron, as the Roman Catholic Church incited public book burning events, called "Bonfires of the Vanities".

The progressive education tradition emphasizes how the education of children and adolescents can build on real-life experience, i.e. learning by doing. Reading and discussing *The Decameron* during the COVID pandemic seemed like a good jumping-off point for multi-faceted learning experiences for adolescents and young adults living in the midst of chaos.

Here are some of the subject areas that could be taught building on what is naturally of interest to young people, especially in a pandemic:

Medical science, genetics, immunology. Schools could invite guest speakers who work on developing vaccines, leading to learning about the science behind different kinds of vaccines, potential problems, etc.

Sociology, political science. There could be learning about the thinking behind anti-vaxxer positions, elaborated in role-played debates and other conversations with an anti-vaxxer; there could be discussion of what can be learned about the role of politics in public health, the parts of the country/world most likely to favor vaccines and other public health approaches, including a role-played debate with someone who's against/for a role for government.

Discussion of the popularity of Andrew Tate and Jordan Peterson, in the context of polarized politics turbo-charged by the pandemic.

Literature and the arts. Decameron; "Hamnet" by Maggie O'Farrell.

European history, the bonfire of the vanities. What would it be like to live through a pandemic without a germ theory, without vaccines, why was the Roman Catholic Church so dead set against *The Decameron*?

Another issue that has become newly relevant in a school context had to do with how the COVID crisis was dealt with in schools with progressive educational philosophies. From Dewey (1938) onward, practitioners of progressive education took as a guiding principle that children best learn by doing.

All of the aforementioned themes will require extensive preparation of teachers and other school staff who will be involved in initiating and leading discussion. There will be reluctance and opposition to some aspects of these conversations with children and adolescents. If adult anxiety and differences of opinion with respect to these topics accounts for long-standing avoidance of such conversations, it is likely that in many school settings, it will take months and years before any of these topics can be addressed with children and adolescents. Groups of teachers will have passionately held differences of opinion about masking, vaccinations, etc. The history of sex education in schools provides a cautionary case in point. On the positive side, just as "resistance" turned out to lead seamlessly into the substance of the analytic work, in the end Freud concluded that analysis of resistance (along with analysis of transference) was the very essence of psychoanalysis. Likewise, in many cases it may turn out that discussion of how and why we don't study pandemic history, or any of the topics suggested above, with children and adolescents may be the best lead-in to the study of various aspects of pandemic history.

Psychoanalytic Hospitals

Some clinical programs operate as a community, the community itself a therapeutic agent according to psychoanalytic principles. Some inpatient psychiatric hospitals or units regard themselves this way, such as the Austen-Riggs Center in Stockbridge, Massachusetts, USA, and the erstwhile Chestnut Lodge in Rockville, Maryland, USA. Austen-Riggs continues to function as a long-term inpatient hospital and center of Continuing Education for psychotherapists with a strongly psychoanalytic and eclectic orientation. Chestnut Lodge closed down in 2009 after a lawsuit found it negligent in the care of psychiatric inpatients for failing to include psychotropic medications in treatment plans. In its heyday, Chestnut Lodge had been a prominent center of psychoanalytic theoretical and clinical innovation, with prominent psychoanalytic contributors like Harold Searles (1979), Frieda Fromm-Reichmann (1960), and Harry Stack Sullivan (1953). Stanton and Schwartz (1954), as noted above, conducted a three-year study of long-term hospital treatment at Chestnut Lodge. Among its conclusions, this study found that including patient input in the operation of the hospital was associated with positive therapeutic outcomes. Stanton and Schwartz's findings reinforced other studies in an industrial context that found that worker-functioning in factories benefited from worker participation, as active members of the community, in the running of the factory.

Kernberg (1992) studied a hospital psychiatric unit, identifying group-level defenses with the distortions in functioning they introduced. He discussed the counterproductive effect of granting certain "privileges" to a patient from a wealthy family who pulled strings, insisting on exemption from certain responsibilities on the ward. In this way her pathological narcissism was reinforced.

Main (1989) did a similar study of hospital dynamics. These systemic studies outside of the private office illustrate certain aspects of psychoanalysis at its best: the study of anxiety, defense, collusion in disabling the analytic function and other counterproductive outcomes. Adapting the traditional psychoanalytic model to address family and other systemic challenges was less of a stretch than it might have been elsewhere without the integration of psychoanalytic and systemic foci. Sprince (2002), in a Kleinian and Bionian framework, described her work as a consultant in a residential treatment center where numbing and over-indulgence came to be seen as defenses on the part of the staff against contact with the traumatic experiences that the adolescents brought to their treatments. Sprince herself comments that even twice removed as she was from these traumatic experiences, she found herself "frequently terrified". Putting her own experience, along with that of the staff and the patients, in this sort of context enabled a capacity to think that allowed all involved to avoid destructive acting out. Here again, we see a useful confluence of psychoanalytic and systemic thinking.

See Altman, 2015, pp. 85–86 for more discussion of psychoanalytic work in hospital communities.

Community Trauma: Clinical Intervention, Research, Primary Prevention

Beatrice Beebe (2001; Beebe & Lachmann, 2002; Beebe et al., 2005; Beebe et al., 2012; Beebe et al., 2016, *inter alia*) is a clinician and theoretician who also leads a research team at the Columbia University Medical Center. Her research focuses on mother-infant social communication and the development of attachment patterns. Her research and clinical interests are extraordinarily wide-ranging. In the present context, we will focus on her community-focused project in New York City following the attacks of September 11, 2001. The community concerned was New York City, a city of millions, not to mention the traumatic ripples that engulfed the nation and the world. This research identified a pattern of hypervigilant interaction between traumatized mothers and their babies, leading to intervention strategies to modulate anxiety-ridden efforts on the part of mothers to repair ruptures with their babies instantly. Intervention aimed to help the mothers tolerate normal moments of disruption, avoiding exacerbation of anxiety and insecurity in both mother and baby. Ultimately the procedure aimed to support the mothers in embarking on a normal grieving process.

This project addressed a community trauma. Beebe and her colleagues identified a shared response that threatened to build a developmental distortion into a transgenerational cycle. The rationale for the intervention was based in psychoanalytic developmental theory based on attachment research; it thus qualifies as a full-fledged example of Community Psychoanalysis. No couch, no discrete individual as patient, normal, understandable responses to a community-wide trauma as presenting problem. There are many such projects: in war zones, in neonatal nurseries (Kraemer, 2006; Kraemer & Steinberg, 2006; Steinberg 2006) and beyond.

In this section so far, we have explored how links between individual psychoanalysis and Community Psychoanalysis were forged as concepts and dynamics, mostly defensive in nature like projective identification and dissociation, proved applicable both to individuals and to large and small groups. Differences in underlying theories of therapeutic action between individual psychoanalysis and psychotherapy, and group analysis, having become more blurred, the rationale for a hard and fast line between in-office "pure gold" psychoanalysis designed to allow for uncontaminated study of transference, and in-or-out of office work with individuals and/or groups have also becomes blurred. These forms of psychoanalytic therapy were brought closer together, united by a common focus on dysfunctional defenses against existential anxieties shared by all human beings. With frame issues thus less crucial in distinctions between psychoanalysis and other forms of psychotherapy, the ability to pay relatively high fees became less of an exclusionary criterion as the doors swung open to people of less economically privileged social and educational status who formerly were excluded based on now-outmoded criteria of analyzability. This shift became more pronounced as the COVID pandemic drove therapists of all stripes out of their office-based 'havens'.

Ecology

Climate change is currently disrupting human and non-human animal life pervasively and, episodically, catastrophically. Hurricanes, floods, wildfires, and heat waves have always been with us, but the relentless rise of insurance premiums provides indisputable evidence of their prevalence and destructiveness. People are moving away from coastal zones; people are dying as temperatures soar to unprecedented levels. Destructive effects of climate change are concentrated in countries and coastal zones where most of the world's population lives, with predictable geopolitical effects coming down the pike. These are ignored for the most part by the rich countries emitting the pollutants fueling the change, unless, of course, they can profit from development of renewable energy sources without disrupting energy-hogging AI data centers.

Bodnar (2004, p. 798) points out how there are seamless links between the states of the ecosystem and internal psychological states when she writes, referring to landscapes: (they) "inhabit us as we inhabit them". Mother earth is our mother, after all. We are fed by sunlight via plants, our bodies are largely composed of river and ocean water. Our mother is being "wasted and bombed" (Bodnar, 2006) as we fail to regulate our consumption of her gifts.

Nicholsen (2002) elaborates beautifully and powerfully on this point. She points out that few people are insensitive and unresponsive to the beauty of nature, but making the link to action intended to cultivate and preserve that beauty is regarded as a niche concern, cut off from the political world where such action can be undertaken. Case in point: as I write in early 2025, the Southern California coast shows what the end of the world would/will look like, while politicians trade blame.

Sangath

In 2015, I (Altman, 2015) wrote about an extraordinary community-based mental health outreach program called "Sangath". Based in Goa, South India, Sangath was, and is, training lay people to reach out, within their own communities, to people who appear to suffer from psychological distress. Outreach workers receive a manual to guide them through the process of interviewing people in distress and referring them to sources of help, only some of which are traditional psychotherapy or pharmacotherapy. Other options encompassed spiritually based practices with which community members and lay outreach workers would likely be familiar, including meditation and breathing exercises. Other recommendations include an eclectic mix of CBT-type interventions, approaches to problem-solving, reassurance, and explanation. Sangath is community-based in a number of ways: patients and practitioners live in the same community, within the same or similar cultural context. Sangath functions in multiple areas of India and other places in the Global South.

In the intervening years since 2015, Sangath's work has disseminated widely on a global basis (see Cohen, Patel & Minas, 2013). Sangath has taken on outcome research (sometimes through digital modalities), applied to a number of clinical entities (sangath.in) guided by principles and values of equity and wide availability to underserved people of all age groups. They present their approaches as evidence-based. There are special programs for people with addictions, cases of domestic violence, and perinatal depression and for people of marginalized sexual groups.

See Altman, 2015, pp. 87–95 for more discussion of Sangath's work around the world.

Ricardo Ainslie: Psychoanalytic Ethnography

Another contributor coming from slightly off the mental health mainstream is Ricardo Ainslie. Ainslie was born and raised in Mexico City, moving to Texas as a young adult. He is Professor in the University of Texas Counseling Psychology program. As a Mexican-American and a Counseling Psychologist, he, like Freud as a Jew, brought a slightly off-center perspective to psychoanalysis.

Ainslie's projects, three of which are summarized below in his own words, fall under the category of what I am calling "Community Psychoanalysis" and what he calls "Psychoanalytic Ethnography". Psychoanalytic Ethnography is a key component in the toolkit of those who practice Community Psychoanalysis, opening up the affect-laden, personal and lived experience of those who spend their lives in the community. Ainslie (2025, personal communication) defines this term as follows:

> By psychoanalytic ethnography I mean taking the tools that we learn as the basis for the therapeutic engagement as psychoanalysts (a disciplined, focused listening strategy, prioritizing the effort to understand the subjectivity of another person while monitoring your own subjective responses and while taking into account your personal history and how it may shape the encounter and the relationship) and using these tools outside of the consulting room with people who are living experiences that you are interested in exploring and understanding. All of these projects have involved interviews and encounters with individuals who don't fit that model in terms of intensity (say, a community historian, or a political figure, or other people who are primarily sources of relevant information), but all have also involved extended, in-depth interviews with people ('key informants' if you will) whose experience of the events or circumstances in question are critical to what I am trying to understand. The latter are more akin to the psychoanalytic treatment situation and those interviews are, in many respects, often indistinguishable from a clinical encounter except for the fact that they are taking place in someone's living room, or on a porch, or in a pickup truck.

Ainslie describes three of his projects as follows:

1 "(My) first book, *No Dancin' in Anson* narrates the impact of the Civil Rights Era on a small Texas town. Mexicans who had only been permitted to live on ranches in the county gradually moved into Anson, Texas (population 2,800), and their children became cheerleaders, bank tellers, and police officers." The controversy over the right to dance (as in the film "Footloose") became a proxy for the deep stresses and conflicts within the community brought on by the era's profound social change. This included the alliances, primarily between individuals of Mexican ancestry and "outsider whites", that formed within the community.
2 There followed "a documentary film, *Crossover: A story of desegregation*, about the experience of school desegregation in Hempstead, Texas (population 3,500), following on the US Civil Rights laws which were enacted in the 1960s. Notwithstanding the gains that were made during this social transformation, they came at a cost to the African-American community, where their Jim Crow-era school, the only place where the entire black community had been able to gather in Hempstead, was razed during the desegregation process and its contents, including prized trophies from regional and state-wide competitions, disappeared. Such was the attempt to erase this school from the community's public memory, that there was no mention of it in the school district's official history. *Crossover* narrates this period in the community, and it became part of a process of "making

conscious what had been unconscious" given the complete erasure of this Black institution and everything associated with it. Prompted by the process of creating the documentary, an advisory committee of the school's former students and teachers came together to organize the first ever reunion of the school's alumni. An event was created in which alumni and teachers "told the story" of their school before an integrated audience of teachers, families, and community leaders. The event became a forum for acknowledging this exiled and repressed history. At the school district offices, a trophy case was installed displaying memorabilia associated with the Jim Crow-era school as a permanent exhibit. All of these elements were informed by the psychoanalytic understanding of the importance of putting one's history into words and the process was led by the local advisory committee. *Crossover* became a training tool used by Humanities Texas (the Texas arm of the National Endowment for the Humanities) to train college students at Historically Black Colleges and Universities (HBCUs) to conduct oral histories of the era of school desegregation in their own communities".

Another episode addressed by Ainslie occurred in 1998:

James Byrd, Jr., a black man, was abducted and dragged to his death behind a pickup truck driven by three white men in Jasper, Texas (population 8,000). The hate crime was a modern-day lynching and it stirred deep anxieties and conflict within the community. The situation was made more volatile in the following days by members of the Black Panthers and Ku Klux Klan who descended on Jasper. (Ainslie's) ethnographic work included extensive interviews with members of the white and Black community, and it documents the psychological impact of this hate crime on the town, as well as recounting the processes by which violence was averted. The Jasper project also resulted in a psychobiography of John William King, the driving force behind the hate crime. King became the first white person since Reconstruction to be sentenced to die in Texas for the murder of a black person (one of the other perpetrators also received the death penalty, while the third received a life sentence).

In all these projects, (Ainslie) focused on a community in danger of unraveling as a polarized collective dynamic threatened to devolve into conflict and, in the case of Jasper, violence. Analogized to psychic unraveling, (Ainslie) and his collaborators embarked on an anti-splitting process that helped restore communication and engagement. In this way, (his) projects help re-form relationships in the communities where he conducted this psychoanalytically informed ethnographic work.

Ainslie comments on how, in these and other projects, psychoanalytic ethnography morphs into a therapeutic intervention.

"In these encounters I am not there to provide therapy, but the experience of these individuals is often therapeutic in that they deeply engage issues and experiences about which they have powerful feelings".

Ainslie thus retraces the footsteps of Sigmund Freud who started out doing research into the pathogenesis of hysteria, ending up with a therapeutic intervention that he called "psychoanalysis".

See Altman, 2015, pp. 59–65 for an extended discussion of Ainslie's work.

Ryan to Parker: How Do White People Represent Slavery?

Ryan Parker's (2019) study of "Slavery in the white psyche" began with a question to her subjects whom she had identified as white (presumably based on their self-identification) about their "memories and experiences of learning about slavery".

"Eleven of the 15 participants recalled" not learning much. "Three participants had no memory whatsoever of learning about slavery in school. As one participant explained, "It wasn't in the textbooks we used; it just was the unspoken. We don't want to go there whether we are proud of that history or not proud of that history" (p. 5).

Parker interprets this and other such statements as evidence of pervasive disavowal of thoughts and feelings about the enslavement of Black people. In the present context I want to highlight the seemingly spontaneous emergence of awareness of this defensive process at work in the group, the "we" (White people) with which she identifies. This is a strikingly analytic, self-reflective outcome of a brief conversation out of "the office", an example of what Ainslie had described as psychoanalytic ethnography: in-depth conversations with "key informants" that concern their experience of life in their community, though not intended to be therapeutic, do focus on clarifying and articulating emotional experience.

An insight-based first step toward a talking cure, indeed.

Parker finds, repeatedly with her subjects, that, though she asks about their experience as White people, they generally focus on what they imagine to have been the experience of Black people, the victims, not the perpetrators. At one point she goes on to ask her subjects: "What do you think it might have been like to be born into a slave-owning family?" (p. 14).

"Upon my asking the question, three participants immediately launched into a fantasy of being a slave or slave child. Three additional participants responded with confusion and immediately paused to ask for clarification:" The family that owns, not the family that's the slave? "This means that over one-third of the participants were so defended against even the fantasy of identification with the slave master, that they struggled to—or simply could not—hear the question" (p. 14).

The defense here is mobilized against the fantasy of acting as the perpetrator, not the victim, of violence and oppression.

Ryan concludes that many White people find it difficult, or impossible, to acknowledge the reality of the race-based harm their people have inflicted. Thus, any sort of reparative action is barely conceivable. It is interesting to note how what looks like empathy with the victim can simultaneously function as a defense against guilt. Guilt, responsibility, and empathy ideally all coexist.

One subject moves toward acknowledging his potential to become a perpetrator, while taking the opportunity to explore why that might be avoided.

> If you were a boy, you would be seeing the whippings of your parents and friends, the brutal whippings. So, clearly you wouldn't want to go there. If you were a girl you probably wouldn't see the beatings and things like that, but maybe as a boy because they would be expected to do that one day; but definitely not the girls, they would not have seen that.
>
> (p. 15)

Self-reflectiveness is seen as a strength across diverse schools of thought in psychoanalysis. In ego-oriented psychoanalysis, self-reflectiveness is a precondition for self-generated change. As Kliman points out (see p. 18 above) self-reflectiveness is a sign of an analytic process at work. Avoidance of self-reflectiveness may, correspondingly, be a manifestation of a generalized defensive process. Parker's encouraging her sample of white-identified subjects to think about the experience of slave owners thus amounts to a kind of "diagnostic" probe eliciting a response that preemptively shuts down self-reflective thinking. Perhaps shame and anticipated disapproval, or self-disapproval, counterproductively reinforces defensiveness (see Altman, 2024, for a discussion of how consciousness-raising groups can elicit defensive responses from White people). The response of the subject just quoted above shows that, at least in some cases, the process initiated by Parker's question can stimulate self-reflectiveness, especially if the researcher is experienced as non-judgmental, as fundamentally curious.

Even more so, from a Kleinian/Bionian perspective, failure to develop thinking capacity is a basic flaw in psychic development and psychic functioning. Bion, elaborating on Klein's theory, opened up the process of transformation of raw reactivity into psychological experience, thoughts and feelings, subjective experience. He called this process "alpha function", close to what later came to be known as "mentalization", a core aspect of distinctively human being, a precondition for the Kleinian depressive position.

Ogden (1986) described a process by which people get locked into the paranoid-schizoid position, in which interpretive subjectivity is not available, in which life events are what they are, unmediated by an interpretive subjectivity. Therapeutic change, analytic progress, depends on people realizing that they are active agents in constructing their experience through their interpretive activity, which can be changed as they become aware of themselves as interpreting subjects. Until that point, life just "is what it is" and "there's no two ways about it", no options, no possibility of therapeutic change.

Melanie Klein thought people get stuck this way when good and bad cannot be reconciled, when things just are what they are and there are no two ways about it. Guilt, about being from a family connected with slavery in Parker's case report, is a dead end, best avoided. Just change the subject.

By inquiring as she did, Parker stimulated thought, which loosened up the impasse, pointing the way toward an exit.

Deepti Sachdev

Deepti Sachdev (2024) studied the relationship between the ancient Indian caste structure and the evolving system of higher education in India. Generally, people of lower caste status are shunted toward manual labor and jobs regarded as polluting. At the other extreme, people of high caste status do intellectual and spiritually ennobling work. In recent years, the Indian government has tried to shake up these hierarchies, making efforts to provide opportunities and reserving places for lower caste people in higher education and academic employment.

Academic achievement is highly valued in India and associated with high social status. Thus, beneficiaries of Indian affirmative action in higher education often feel out of place, defensive about their right to be in a class in a well-regarded university, and insecure both in their home communities and in their places of study. This constellation of feelings has a great deal in common with beneficiaries of affirmative action elsewhere, except that in India the caste system bears the imprimatur of the divine, cosmic, order, set up by the ancient gods, scripturally ordained since time immemorial.

Sachdev narrates and discusses her experience at a university with one of her students, whom she calls Savita. Savita is an energetic and active participant in Sachdev's class but is consumed with anxiety as examinations approach. Sachdev, in this connection learns that she is from the dalit (formerly "untouchable") caste or, rather, outcaste. Sachdev herself is of a high caste. This article is of interest as the anxieties Sachdev describes in herself are both well known to a North American White-Jewish reader like me and, simultaneously, fully embedded in an Indian cultural context. Sachdev describes both Savita's universal-sounding feelings of anxiety about feeling out of place in the university and angry reactions to feeling marginalized in a higher education context, likely drawing on remnants of the Colonial British feeling of superiority when it came to matters of the intellect. Savita and her classmates often turned class discussions away from the assigned focus and toward their feelings about their place in the system.

One day Savita appeared for an examination with an injured wrist. She clearly felt on the defensive, struggling to respond to faculty questions. Some faculty members withdrew into seemingly hostile silence. Sachdev not only felt angry on Savita's behalf but also felt guilty for her role as a faculty member participating in Savita's victimization.

Sachdev links the moral of this story to the idea of identification with the aggressor, originating with Anna Freud (1966), then propounded by Fanon and Ferenczi. Fanon, in his home country of Martinique and later in Algeria, had noted how colonized people identified with the degraded images projected onto them by the colonizers, in this case by Europeans, the French. Surrounded by countless examples of subtle or blatant exploitation and mistreatment of indigenous, "native" people like themselves, degradation gets wired into their self images. Remedial measures like affirmative action in the United States, or reserved spots in employment or education settings in India and elsewhere, creates a disconnect between an internalized feeling of inferiority and an elite external placement. Thus, Savita's discomfort in class, and especially when on the spot, in examinations. Under colonial regimes, degraded images of the colonized serve to justify mistreatment by the colonizers. When the formerly colonized nation is liberated from the colonial system, those who end up on top, in India likely of high caste in the ancient hierarchy, may assume the oppressive position formerly occupied by the French in Africa, for example. Sachdev, in her article, illuminates the position of someone inhabiting such a role, but also educated into an egalitarian value system from which she wants Savita to feel of value, valued. Savita, for her part, is consumed by a struggle with the demons of her deeply implanted sense of worthlessness.

Observing Savita floundering, Sachdev's thoughts turn to an Indian myth, one from the Mahabharata, of Elkavya and Dhronacharya. Elkavya, wishing to become a great archer, goes to a teacher of archery, a guru named Dhronacharya, to advance his skills. Dhronacharya rejects Elkavya's request, comparing him unfavorably to another of his students, the renowned Arjuna. He demands a fee from Elkavya nonetheless, his right thumb which must be severed. This is, obviously, a seriously disabling injury for an archer. Elkavya complies even though he does not receive the desired service from Dhronacharya. Elkavya tries to overcome this disability by pulling on the bowstring with his forefinger and middle finger, succeeding with a handicap, like Savita.

The interpretation of this myth would require a book in itself. Be that as it may, with this myth in mind, Sachdev worries that faculty, including herself, may unconsciously throw up roadblocks to the success of someone like Savita, suffering from guilt-induced conflict about their own social progress in postcolonial India, requiring students to cut off crucial resources, like fingers. The culturally specific point may be that devotion to teachers is a supreme value, even when it seems that extreme sacrifice is required. In the end, sacrifice may be the royal road to learning and mastery.

Parenthetically at this point, but critically in the evolution of psychoanalysis, Ferenczi (1933) similarly applied the idea of identification with the aggressor to the development of sexually and otherwise abused children, casting light on how the abused might become the abuser in later life. Finally, also parenthetically and critically, Sachdev's linkage of an ancient Indian myth with a psychoanalytic concept establishes rootedness for psychoanalysis across centuries and continents.

Sudhi Kakar and Ashis Roy: Perspectives on India from the Indian Subcontinent

In the context of increasing polarization and alienation between and among identity-based groups around the world, Indian psychoanalyst Ashis Roy undertook a study of intimate Hindu-Muslim relationships in India. The Indian community is currently split by the forces of "Hindutva", i.e. Hindu dominance, in the context of a huge Muslim minority and a history of peaceful coexistence interspersed with episodes of violence, among which is the partition of India and Pakistan in which a million people were killed.

Roy's starting point is a confluence of the studies of identity by Erik Erikson and Sudhir Kakar. Kakar makes a key distinction between identity based on "wholeness", in which diverse elements interact with mutual respect, and identity based on "totality", in which one element seeks to dominate. Roy quotes Kakar:

> Wholeness seems to connote an assembly of parts, even quite diversified parts, that enter into fruitful association and organization—"Totality on the contrary evokes a Gestalt in which an absolute boundary is emphasized: given a certain arbitrary delineation, nothing that belongs inside is to be left outside, nothing that must be outside can be tolerated inside" (Roy, 2024, p. 16).

Roy's narrative starts with the long history, through centuries, of "wholeness" in Indian identity, with Hinduism and Islam forming an assembly of parts, often quite fruitful, recently disassembled by the partition between India and Pakistan and subsequent episodic violence. Roy's book amounts to a Community Psychoanalytic intervention as he inquires into how intimate partners navigate the force field formed by these ways of navigating difference and similarity in intimate relationships. Marriages in India traditionally are arranged on a family basis; the baseline situation reinforces segregation based on castes and communities. Meanwhile, "love marriages" occur, they always have, but out of the light cast by open discussion. Roy's book, drawing on Kakar's work, a mix of fiction and nonfiction, drawing parallels between identity dynamics in intimate spaces, with identity dynamics on a large socio-political level. All this is refracted through a psychoanalytic lens, illuminating and provoking thought on many levels.

Honey Oberoi Vahali and Tibetan Refugees

In these days of forced deportations and refugees walking long distances seeking asylum, the experience of Tibetan refugees has a special resonance. Subject to discrimination, oppression, and torture after Tibet was forcibly annexed by China in 1959, many Tibetans, accompanied by their spiritual and political leader, the Dalai Lama, walked over the highest mountain range on earth, the Himalayas, eventually settling in and around Dharamsala, India. There they became a nation within a nation. Tibetans speak their own language and have their own governmental leadership (the Dalai Lama). They are largely Buddhists, in a Hindu, Muslim, and Christian context (Buddhism is widely recognized as having Hindu roots). They live within India, always hoping some day to return to Tibet. The Indian community has many sub-communities, but few as distinct as Tibetans.

It speaks to the traditional Indian sense of inclusiveness that Vahali (2009) the Director of the School of Human Studies at an Indian governmental university would devote herself to listening to the experiences of Tibetans before, during, and after exile, in their own words. Vahali is extraordinary, even in an Indian context for her openness to the experiences of marginalized people, exemplified in a decades-long relationship with a dalit (formerly "untouchable") community in Delhi.

Vahali is especially attuned to the nonviolent strands in the Buddhist way of life that influences Tibetan feelings about the Chinese. She feels that responding to violence with violence, for both perpetrator and victim, is corrupting for all concerned. In fact, she indicates that experience being "victimized" may promote spiritual development to the extent that one learns to resist the ultimately futile pull toward violence. As Gandhi taught: an eye for an eye leaves everyone blind. This ethical point of view may discourage violence, such as terrorism, but Vahali indicates (personal communication, 2019) that some in the younger generation, living in India, are becoming impatient with restraint, and abstention from violence, toward the Chinese.

What stands out in Vahali's approach is that she *listens* to her Tibetan subjects. She wants to see the world from their point of view. She does not seek objective knowledge, disconnected from empathy. Years ago, as she passed by a "basti" ("slum" community) on her walk to her office, her curiosity drew her to take the initiative to meet its occupants.

On one of my visits to Delhi, Vahali and I planned to co-teach a graduate school class about life in the bastis. One day before the class was to start, she said to me that she felt we would not be able to teach such a class until we, she and I, had some firsthand experience in a basti. She proposed that we, including us both and all our students, should go out and have a conversation with someone whom we would normally avoid. Then each student, including Honey and me, would report back to the entire group on our experience, with feedback from the group.

See Altman, 2015, pp. 19–20, 22–24, 30–42 for some of these experiences. The main point here is that Vahali felt that immersing ourselves in a personal way in the communities and with the people about whom we were presuming to teach would be insurance against distancing ourselves through objectification.

4 Evolving Psychoanalytic Theory

Language, Individualism, Society, and Culture

Even in the United States, the more extreme and uncompromising individualism of classical psychoanalysis had to make room for psychoanalytic engagement with the social world on clinical and social levels. Interpersonal psychoanalysis spearheaded by Harry Stack Sullivan (1953) and Erich Fromm (1956) and under the influence of Sándor Ferenczi in Europe took hold in the United States. As the focus of mainstream versions of psychoanalysis expanded to include the social world in one way or another, others doubled down on deepening the focus on individual experience. The result was such an incoherence in the meaning of "psychoanalysis" that the various strands or foci hardened into nearly uncrossable boundaries, comparable to disciplinary boundaries like the boundaries between ethnic studies, sociology, and the study of religion and spirituality. Many of these sub-disciplines continued to lay claim to the label or "brand" of psychoanalysis. The word "psychoanalysis" had a powerful hold on the culture; no one wanted to abandon the brand, leaving it to others. Sigmund Freud had a powerful vision and had applied his vision to a wide swath of disciplines, from medicine to sociology to history, including the history of religion, to psychology, and beyond; He had succeeded in claiming such a huge territory for psychoanalysis that his heirs had to deal with the alternative and competing claims of adjacent disciplines across academia. To advance the field, his heirs had their work cut out for them! In this book I am addressing one piece of that huge task: an overview of efforts on the part of Freud's heirs to address an exclusivity of psychoanalysis that undercut his ambition to construct a universally applicable psychology.

This goal ran afoul of Freud's wish and need to control the development of psychoanalysis. Freud's followers, who differed with him on key theoretical or technical points, such as Adler, Jung, and Ferenczi, ran the risk of excommunication, despite Freud's repeated tendency to differ with himself, to revise his own work, as his active mind ceaselessly innovated.

One of the first challenges to Freud's control of psychoanalysis emerged from India, as we have already noted, where Girindrasekhar Bose dared to

DOI: 10.4324/9781003661146-5

differ with Freud by claiming that the Oedipus complex as Freud described it did not unfold in India in the way Freud envisioned it. There were many analysts trying to help Freud extricate himself from the corner into which he had painted himself. Britten (1992), like Lacan (1978) and Ogden (1986), wrote about the Oedipal situation as the time of "thirdness" when the mother-child dyad gets broken up by the father, the third, the other. Dyads, the analytic dyad, the mother-child dyad, are now framed by the external space, a third space, surrounding them. The problem is: they always were. To take full account of this fact, one needs some form of systems theory, something like Community Psychoanalysis. A dyadic point of view isn't excluded by a triadic or systemic perspective; the more inclusive perspective subsumes the less inclusive one(s).

Now let's see what happens when one tries to build a stand-alone system, a one- or two-person theory, like classical Freudian psychoanalysis, and what happens when one tries to add a third term.

In the case of psychoanalysis, what happened was that, growing out of Freud's insistence on controlling the evolution of psychoanalysis, a series of polarizing arguments broke out over what was "really" psychoanalysis and what was not. Those of us who tried, in conferences, to present community-based psychoanalysis as truly psychoanalytic faced rooms full of people protesting that while the work we had done was all well and good, even helpful, it was NOT psychoanalysis.

A variation of this theme was that classically minded people thought that "interpersonal psychoanalysis" was an oxymoron. A number of classically minded people, Freudian and Kleinian, claimed that proponents of their point of view had *always* taken account of the influence, the impact, of the other person in the room, i.e. the analyst. Interpersonal psychoanalysis was nothing new, or perhaps it was not psychoanalysis. Freudian-inclined people thought that a proper stance or analytic frame could establish guard rails around the analyst's *personal* participation in such a way that at some basic level the uncontaminated focus on the patient remained intact. Adherents of Kleinian/ Bionian psychoanalysis introduced the idea of "projective identification" to acknowledge that the patient's transference in the form of projections onto the analyst did, indeed, have a personal impact on the analyst. But these Kleinian/ Bionian adherents insisted that the impact of the patients' projections could be confined to a space of "reverie" so that it could be used in the service of understanding the patient without contaminating the analyst's objectivity.

The Fly in the Ointment

It was not lost on Freud that the analytic situation was and is potentially a setup for exploitation of the patient by the analyst, sexually and otherwise. The patient in the early years of psychoanalysis was usually a young woman. The analyst was a middle-aged man. Their society was patriarchal. Freud's case of

Dora (Freud, 1905) is famously a case in point. Dora was a teenage girl whose father was having an extramarital affair with Frau K, the wife of Herr K. A plan was afoot to buy off Herr K by setting Dora up to have an affair with Herr K. But Dora rejected Herr K's advances instead developing hysterical symptoms. Dora was sent to Freud for treatment of those symptoms by psychoanalysis.

It did not occur to Freud that Dora's symptoms were an outgrowth of her feeling that she, and indeed Freud himself, were pawns in her father's game. Freud interpreted to Dora that her symptoms arose from her feeling sexually overstimulated by Herr K's advances. Dora refused to continue the analysis with Freud. In a postscript to the case report, Freud speculated that Dora's refusal arose from unrecognized negative transference, but it did not occur to him that Freud's collusion with the exploitation of Dora, a kind of attempted parallel seduction, formed a realistic basis for her refusal to continue with both Freud and Herr K.

Over time, as patriarchal culture came into focus as enabling exploitation of women, it became clear that there were undercurrents of a sexual and romantic nature flowing strongly in the typical analytic situation. Freud's and his followers' insistence on the detached objectivity of the analyst amounted to an over-reaction in the effort to keep these undercurrents underground. Breuer's way of handling his patient Anna O's declaration of love for him, along with her false claim to have become pregnant by him, is a prime example of this counterproductive overreaction. Breuer terminated the analysis with Anna O and went on vacation with his wife. Freud continued analytic work with Anna O, in the process developing the idea of transference. Given the number of Freud's other followers (Ferenczi, Jung, among others) who reportedly had sexual and romantic liaisons with their patients, it appears that this effort was significantly unsuccessful in fostering ethical behavior. The irony is that the concept of "enactment" in psychoanalysis offered a way out: a way to acknowledge the inevitability of ethically questionable sexual and romantic *feelings* along with fantasies and impulses in the psychoanalytic situation while maintaining an ethically based restraint ruling out putting such fantasies and impulses into action.

It cannot be denied that restraint of sexual impulses, once aroused, poses a more difficult and complicated challenge than restraint of other impulses, such as angry or rageful impulses. In psychoanalysis, which inherently needs to focus on sexual feelings, talking can be arousing in itself, to the point where the boundary between talking and doing can be difficult to define and maintain. Total restraint can seem to make sense as a strategy to avoid a slippery slope of temptation. Thus, the emphasis on abstinence in the psychoanalytic frame or in the living arrangements of monks and nuns. On the other hand, too much restraint in itself can be counterproductive. As Ghent (1991) pointed out the appeal of surrender is only increased by holding back the beast.

So unqualified abstinence is not the key for psychoanalysts. The enactments that occur around sexual desire, focusing on the interplay of subjectivities, offers a third way, not an inevitable slippery slope. The sexual desire of human beings is undeniably a powerful force, but not the only powerful one. Narcissism, curiosity, the need for love, for recognition, for self-expression, masochistic and sadistic impulses, all come into play.

When I was a candidate in psychoanalytic training a male instructor said a female patient once said: "I want to get on the floor and make passionate love with you". The analyst said, "Why the floor?"

To me, the analyst was showing that he was not overcome by the need to surrender and had not given up his capacity for curiosity and analytic exploration. The content remained sexual but the nature of the enactment had been transformed. If the analyst had been silent, paralyzed, with or without abstinence as rationale, the interaction might have been experienced by one or both participants as depriving and/or seductive.

The Impact of Edgar Levenson, Merton Gill and Interpersonal Psychoanalysis

Edgar Levenson (1972) posited that the action level of a verbal intervention is "isomorphic" with the content. In other words action recapitulates, action is a "transform" of the verbal content. For example, if you say that someone is sensitive (content), you are likely to hurt their feelings (action). To this, I would add that the meaning in question is not fixed or obvious; it is always ambiguous, open to varying interpretations. The assumption of isomorphism may guide efforts at meaning-making as one seeks a plausible resonance of meaning between words and the action they perform. In other words there is always slippage between the various meanings to which one attributes resonance between content and action. Settling on a particular way in which content and action are presumed to reflect each other, in itself, can shape and reinforce the interaction and the way it is understood. Within this hall of mirrors, slippage between semantic and performed meaning, while potentially confusing, also introduces a potential for change as meaning-making evolves. In all forms of dialogue, including analytic dialogue to the extent that we are open minded, we discover that we are up to more than we thought or something a little different. The unfolding of meaning proceeds unpredictably, though understandable or discussable in retrospect.

Consider the following illustrative example: An analysand floats consideration of a move to a different location with a new lover whose job is moving. Freud had written (1937) that major life changes, like taking a new lover, or a move, should be postponed during an analysis. (In those days a typical analysis might have lasted a few weeks or months.) The analyst, all things considered, proposes that (maybe) this is a case of anxiety-driven flight from the analysis of a currently active transference feeling, perhaps a feeling of being constrained, even trapped. Such an interpretation if spoken (or just thought?) might well contribute to making the analysand feel trapped, which may reinforce the analyst's initial hunch, or perhaps might lead to the analyst's reconsideration of that initial hunch. (How open minded is the analyst? Characterologically, or with this particular analysand at this particular moment?)

In my view, Levenson's point leads to the conclusion that there is no such thing as one-person psychoanalytic psychology. No matter how hard the analyst tries to fade into anonymity or abstinence, that effort in itself is a form of interaction, of participation via the effort not to participate. One could easily go so far as to conclude that efforts not to participate have an *especially* powerful impact on both patient and analyst.

Levenson established that the analyst's participation in an interaction with the analysand is inevitable and most often unconscious. The form that the analyst's participation takes is best knowable in retrospect and deducible from the analysand's reaction. Merton Gill (1983) took a critical step in this regard when he wrote that transference is, in general, a plausible response to the behavior of the analyst. The word "plausible" is key. The analysand is not any more an objective reader of the analyst's feelings than anyone else, but neither is the analysand's perception to be dismissed, as Freud did, by assuming that the analysand's response is a fantasy deriving from the past. The line between past-derived fantasy and realistic perception derived from the present is blurred. The meaning of the behavior of both analyst and analysand is subject to interpretation. To pretend otherwise is anti-analytic.

Could one, must one, extrapolate to the point of claiming that the social environment surrounding the dyad is *also* inevitably influential and must be taken account of in any truly analytic work? I believe that the current predicament of psychoanalysis is evidence that the attempted exclusion of the social surround is not tenable and that such an attempt is decidedly anti-psychoanalytic.

Inherent in the concept of "free association" is the idea that if particular material is excluded in analysis the result could be to undermine an essential "freedom". The social status of patient and analyst, including class, race, gender, religion, and other social factors, is part of the raw material out of which transference and other emotional reactions are constructed. Most fundamentally, curiosity is the driving force of exploration, psychoanalytic exploration in particular. Ruling out of bounds the macro- and micro-social domain hobbles the analytic process, especially in days such as these when society is evolving and changing so profoundly. This book, and others like it, shows that, after decades of inattention to the social domain in psychoanalysis, the chickens have come home to roost.

Theories are filters through which analysts perceive the meaning of their analysands' responses to them. Since there is no final and singular truth in this domain, no particular theory has infallible truth value. Multiple theories are all potentially useful. The analyst is responsible for doing their best to understand with the tools at their disposal.

Comparative Theory: Intrapsychic, Interpersonal, and Systemic Factors All Have a Place in Psychoanalysis, but Differently Prioritized

Is it possible to have a psychoanalytic systemic theory in which intrapsychic, interpersonal, and macro-systemic factors all have a place, all the while working from a fundamentally intrapsychic, or interpersonal, or macro-social systemic, perspective? Is this a contradiction? Or perhaps a paradox? Can we have our cake and eat it too? On a number of occasions, following Greenberg and Mitchell (1983) I have claimed that drive theory and relational theory are mutually inconsistent, that each theory is capable of explaining the same data in its own terms. For example, one could pose the question as to whether sexual attraction follows where love has blazed a trail, or whether love is the handmaiden of sexual attraction. Freud's drive theory makes sexual attraction primary. Loving feelings are derivative of libido, of the sexual drive. Fromm's "Art of Loving" by way of contrast describes love as a relation of mutual respect and valuation. Freudians might counter that the phenomena Fromm describes are *derivative* of libido, that Fromm's love is sublimated libido, or, in the language of ego psychology, has attained a degree of autonomy from drive, drawing on "neutralized" drive energy. In this way, an effort was made to have the cake and eat it too. A variation on this theme was suggested by Kohut in developing his theory of "narcissistic libido", entailing an expansion of the notion of libido so that idealization, infatuation, and such feelings were defined as derivative of a redefined notion of drive.

Kernberg's (1992) conception of idealization is diametrically opposed to Kohut's. Kernberg's Kleinian-derived view is that idealization is defensive against aggression, thus his recommendation to therapists to interpret the underlying aggressive attack on the idealized object. Nothing could be more counterproductive from the perspective of a self psychologist who sees idealization as a fundamental need, who sees extreme idealization as indicating a thwarted need. A relationally oriented therapist might be inclined to consider extreme idealization as a form of enactment, inducing the analyst to expect the other shoe to drop, thus actualizing the kind of outcome predicted by Kernberg.

The key to the seeming paradox here is that the various approaches operate on distinct levels of abstraction. These levels are distinct at a relatively abstract level, at the level of theory. This is the level at which practitioners identify with schools of thought, or general clinical approaches, such as family therapy, or psychoanalysis, or cognitive behavioral therapy. Within these approaches are subgroups. For example, within psychoanalysis, there are intrapsychically oriented analysts, interpersonalists, relationalists, self psychologists, and so on. It is at this high level of abstraction that the various approaches can be seen as mutually incompatible. If you make an appointment for an initial consultation with a family therapist, you will be asked to attend the consultation with your family, the therapist will be assessing the family systemically and will be considering various forms of systemic intervention. If you request a consultation with a psychoanalyst, you will be asked to attend as an individual. The therapist will be making an assessment of you as an individual, considering various individual-level strategies of intervention. Again, schools of thought lead to mutually inconsistent ways of thinking and approaches to intervention. Working with families, one sees individual people as cogs in a wheel. Family therapy interventions are aimed at the wheel as a whole, the family as a system (as in: clarify the lines of authority in the family).

In practice, however, it is often not possible to keep conceptually distinct approaches separate. The individual who made the appointment shows up with the whole family. The therapist invites the family, but one individual shows up.

Even at a more abstract level, it is generally not possible to keep conceptually distinct approaches separate. The level of systems (family systems, socioeconomic systems, and so on) encompasses the level of individual people, but there is an interaction between various levels, e.g. systemic characteristics and individual characteristics. For example, the oppositional personality of one individual interacts with a rigid authority structure in the family. As a therapist, do you aim to encourage flexibility in the rigid individual, or do you try to loosen up the system, i.e. the authority structure of the family? Or both? How?

At this level of intervention, regardless of the therapist's affiliation with a school of thought, it is not only possible to have your cake and eat it too, it is necessary to have the flexibility to juggle both an awareness of the way the family rigidity provokes the individual's oppositionalism, while the individual's oppositionalism provokes the family's rigidity.

There are many critical advantages to a multi-level perspective, allowing for the effects of an intervention at other levels from the one at which it was aimed. For example, therapeutic efforts to enhance the autonomy of an individual adolescent child, which has an individual developmental rationale, may undermine parental authority, which may need to be bolstered by other means. In short, ideally, all practitioners need to be capable of taking an overview perspective of different levels of analysis and the various and complex ways they intersect and interact. But at the moment of acting (making a comment, interpreting, rescheduling, refusing to reschedule, raising the fee, keeping the fee as is, etc.) the range of potential options instantaneously collapses into the one option chosen. But the range of possible meanings, to patient and analyst, also instantaneously opens up at the moment of action. Is raising the fee at a particular moment an act of exploitation? Is it "sanitized" by making it into a routine act, i.e. making the effective date the first of the next month or the next year? The patient and analyst may make different meanings of any given act, and that meaning may change from moment to moment if and when it is discussed.

To add an additional layer of complexity, various individual practitioners with their various personalities have different preferences and different training, thus different starting points in their understanding of the sources of a problem as well as different starting points in planning an intervention.

To sum up, all practitioners (especially beginning practitioners) need a coherent framework in order to address complex clinical realities. They also need the flexibility that derives from access to multiple frameworks in order to address complex multi-layered clinical realities. Additionally, multiple perspectives provide for the emergence of altogether new points of view as they slip and slide over each other.

Fred Pine (1990) in *Drive, Ego, Object, Self* brought together what he called four psychoanalytic psychologies. His framework makes room for the kind of flexibility that I have in mind, but they err, in my view, by assuming that the clinician can choose objectively which perspective best fits a particular patient or a particular clinical situation. Different therapists may have different perspectives with the same individual or the same family. Adopting one theory-based perspective may itself produce confirmatory data. Positing Oedipal rivalry may induce oppositional disagreement, interpretable as competitive, or submissive compliance likewise interpretable. The fit with the subjectivity of the analyst must also be taken into account, the analyst's preferred way of thinking, for example.

5   COVID

The Pandemic Drives Analysts Out of their Offices, into The "Community"

In March 2020, the COVID pandemic suddenly drove psychotherapists out of their offices. This situation forced all psychotherapists to shift gears, but especially psychoanalysts whose way of working largely depended on the particular conditions provided by a private office: a couch to lie on, nearly complete privacy, avoidance of face-to-face contact, and avoidance of informal conversation. In recent decades these requirements of the analytic "frame" have been relaxed to a degree as its rationale was more or less rethought. Nonetheless, therapists who had been trained by analysts, even decades ago, felt uncomfortable with what was often unavoidable spontaneous social interaction.

A subset of analysts had long been uncomfortable with the austerity of the analytic situation and the elitism it generated. On the margins of the psychoanalytic community were anti-elitist, social justice-minded analysts who took pride in departing from the strict frame to work "in the community", on the street with homeless people, in schools, hospitals, Community Mental Health Centers.

The analysts who had their offices pulled out from under their feet were not without a tradition on the margins of their field to fall back on if they so chose. The term "Community Psychoanalysis", however, contains so many contradictions and paradoxes that one wonders how two analysts discussing the topic can agree on the boundaries of their conversation. To many classically minded psychoanalysts, "Community Psychoanalysis" sounds like an oxymoron. For them, psychoanalysis inherently involves two people, one, the analysand, free associating, and the other, the analyst, interpreting the unconscious meaning of the analysand's associations. Ideally, if not essentially, stimuli from outside the analytic dyad are reduced so that the analysand's associations can be taken as reflecting endogenously produced transference in as pure a form as possible. To this end, the private office setting provided the required isolation from extraneous distractions. So, how could therapy conducted out of an office, in the street, with little protection from outside stimulation and not necessarily organized around one

DOI: 10.4324/9781003661146-6

person interpreting the hidden meaning of the other's associations, qualify as "psychoanalysis"?

On the other hand, what might it mean to refer to any form of psychoanalysis as non-community based? Doesn't the traditional office exist within a community? Isn't a community in this context defined to a degree by its public, outside-the-private-office location? Or is a community in this context meant to refer to the socioeconomic and racial diversity of its inhabitants? If so, does the privacy of the private office imply an exclusivity and uniformity of its inhabitants? Perhaps the term "Community Psychoanalysis" is meant to highlight a *relative* exclusivity and uniformity of psychoanalysis conducted in "the office" while recognizing that it never quite works out that way. Embedded in the idea of "Community Psychoanalysis", there seems to reside a protest and a wish to conceive of a more flexible version of psychoanalysis. If so, those who do not use the term or identify with the wish, refrain from acknowledging that Community Psychoanalysis with all its irregularities and unpredictabilities, which is indeed a form of psychoanalysis.

The wish to engage people in a less exclusionary way resides in analysts who seemingly seek economic privilege and social prestige full time, just as the lust for wealth and power is to be found just beneath the surface in even the seemingly most altruistic people. The job of a psychoanalyst is to look beneath the surface, whatever is hiding there. The San Francisco Bay Area has a rich history of social consciousness and has been particularly responsive to community-based psychoanalysis within the United States, alongside its receptivity to the billionaires of Silicon Valley. For all that, The Psychoanalytic Institute of Northern California (PINC), a member Institute of the International Psychoanalytic Association but not of the American Psychoanalytic Association, was all the while sponsoring regular meetings involving representatives of community-based clinics and agencies, with PINC faculty to develop ideas about what institute-community collaboration might look like. Some people at PINC were also floating ideas about training candidates in community-based psychoanalysis.

Evolution of Kleinian/Bionian Theory

A clinical case reported by Brenman-Pick (1985/1988) illustrates an essentially analytic process from a Kleinian/Bionian point of view. If we agree that the process in this case embodies the essence of psychoanalytic inquiry, it is worth asking: What sort of frame makes this sort of process possible? What sort of frame would impede or rule out such an inquiry?

In this case, the patient reports an auto accident on his way to the session in which he narrowly escapes injury. Badly shaken up, he nonetheless reports the facts of the accident dispassionately, including the fact that when he tried to tell his mother about what happened, she said "I don't want to hear about it". Brenman-Pick then proceeds to a commentary on this interaction that encompasses most, if not all, of a Kleinian/Bionian approach to psychoanalysis:

She hears the patient's narrative about the accident, despite its factual basis, as a commentary on the patient' experience of the transference-countertransference interaction. Thus, it illustrates the interdependence of internal and external reality which underlies the whole idea of Community Psychoanalysis.

Brenman-Pick goes on to quote Klein (1952): "in the infant's mind" (i think this statement can apply to all ages), every external experience is interwoven with his phantasies, and—-every phantasy contains elements of actual experience (Brenman-Pick, 1985/1988, p. 36).

In this case, the analyst weaves together *her* experience of the patient's narrative, with the patient's experience of the interaction with his mother.

> The patient made an impact in his 'competent' way of dealing with his feelings. Yet he also conveyed a wish for there to be an analyst/ mother who would take in his fear and his rage——; this supposes the transference on to the analyst of a more understanding maternal figure. I believe, though, that this 'mates' with some part of the analyst that may wish to 'mother' the patient. If we cannot take in and think about such a reaction in ourselves, we either act out by indulging the patient with actual mothering (this may be done in verbal or other sympathetic gestures) or we may become so frightened of doing this, that we freeze and do not reach the patient's wish to be mothered.
>
> (p. 38)

Having thus worked through in the countertransference (the title of the chapter is "Working through in the countertransference"), Brenman-Pick goes on:

> I then needed to show him that in presenting me with such an awful picture of mother/analyst, he persuaded me to believe that I was different from and better than them. Yet he also believed (and that was how he behaved toward me at the beginning of the session) that I too did not want to know about the fear engendered either by unexpected accidents or by the impact he believed he had upon me.
>
> (p. 38)

Note the way Brenman-Pick has to play with language here to convey the blurry boundaries between herself and her patient and her patient's mother (she refers to this conglomerate as "mother/analyst" yet a moment later refers to "mother/analyst" as "them" even though she herself is the analyst!)

The analytic process here depends on the creation of a split-image of the analyst. The analyst is the one from whom the patient needs/wishes for "mothering". At the same time the analyst must stand aside to be able to comment on what is regarded as a core anxiety around the analyst's response to this need/wish. What is needed is a moment in which the need/wish and the analyst's response is suspended in the air between the two people so that they can look at the situation, in all its anxiety-arousing ramifications, together. Here is where the frame must enable a moment of reflection *in media res*. What is needed is to tolerate the missing mothering, the missing "sympathetic gesture", without being so frightened of the patient's response to being deprived that the analyst "freezes", foreclosing the patient's moment of need/wish. The frame must make possible a space between indulgence and deprivation for both parties, a space in which the analyst must feel the temptation to act as a better mother, while suspending action. In that fragile space, that fragile moment, a core anxiety of both parties must be held for joint reflection, likely without words, holding at bay the temptation to resolve the anxiety with indulgence or deprivation, while fully feeling the dilemmas of the moment associated with the symbolic significance of the car accident and the failed maternal response. Is the exquisite hothouse of the office necessary to capture this moment? Could that happen in the raucous street?

If we take this vignette as illustrating an ideal analytic interaction, in which transference-countertransference dynamics can be suspended as if in mid-air for analytic reflection, under what conditions can this sort of analytic moment be cultivated? The question of the moment is whether the hothouse of a private office is a necessary precondition? If so, can analytic reflection occur when analyst and analysand are forced out of the office and into the street?

It is worth noting that the "manifest content" of the session is an event that occurred outside the office, then brought into the analytic space. Can other such outside events be brought into an analytic space constructed for that purpose outside the office?

6   In the Wake of COVID

Existing Community Psychoanalysis projects in the United States, such as they were, became newly salient in the light of conditions brought about by the COVID pandemic. These had been nearly invariably staffed by unpaid volunteers. As a result a split developed between high-fee psychoanalysis and low- or no-fee psychoanalysis, between psychoanalysis for the wealthy and otherwise elite and psychoanalysis "for the people" (Starr & Aron, 2013). To be sure, some practitioners have tried to bridge the gap by reserving some hours for low-fee patients in an otherwise high-fee practice or for unpaid work in the public sector. This is the situation that prevails in law practice, where partners in high-fee firms are expected to devote time to "pro bono" work; it is commonly a mark of status in the corporate world for highly paid executives to serve unpaid on not-for-profit boards. Overall, however, a split between high-fee psychoanalysis in private practice and low-fee or unpaid work in the public sector created a "noblesse oblige" situation that may reinforce the marginal or denigrated status of community-based psychoanalysis. What was, and is, missing is an emphasis on fund-raising in the public and private sectors to pay clinicians to do work out of the office.

Just before the pandemic forced clinicians out of their offices and into the streets, a philanthropist offered a grant to psychoanalytic organizations that were interested in developing a clinical outreach project aimed at undomiciled people in Oregon. The Oregon philanthropist's donation to fund clinical work with people on the street offered an opportunity to develop a model for privately sourced, but non-fee-based, money, for provision of community-based psychoanalytic services. A working group was formed to develop the outreach project and to learn from the experience of trying to put it to work. But the working group that managed the Oregon project never gave serious consideration to paying the clinicians. Their time seeing patients was assumed to be donated time. The opportunity to consult with the "Sunday group", as the working group planning the project and teaching the associated seminar was called, was tacitly assumed to substitute for monetary payment.

Since the clinicians were not being paid, their time spent on this project was taken from weekend time, so as not to displace paid-for time. In many

DOI: 10.4324/9781003661146-7

cases what was displaced was family time or leisure time. It seemed that paid time enjoyed a privileged, untouchable, status. People who had young children or who wanted family time or simply down time on Sundays were thus in a bind with respect to the time the Sunday group, and often the seminars themselves required. A possible long-term resolution that was never seriously considered was to use donated money or to fund-raise to enable payment for time spent serving Community Psychoanalysis so that this work could more easily become part of a clinician's paid-for practice, whether that took the form of clinical work, teaching, or administration.

By sequestering Community Psychoanalytic work into weekends in a capitalist context, the project unwittingly colluded with, and reinforced, the marginalization of Community Psychoanalysis, in terms of its value and its values. This positioning of Community Psychoanalysis was consistent with its frame (improvisational, flexible, emotionally responsive) in contrast with the classical frame (fixed times, time-based fee structure, office-based location, reserved and controlled emotionality). APSA's effort to bring Community Psychoanalysis into the psychoanalytic mainstream was, to a significant but unspoken degree, undermined by its positioning alongside other "non-work" and unpaid activities such as child care, other familial care, and other leisure activities. The "pure gold" version of psychoanalysis was real work despite the availability of funds that could have contributed to placing Community Psychoanalysis into the capitalist mainstream, clinicians' time bought and paid for like office-based private practice.

Another strand of community-oriented psychoanalysis was located in several programs offering free therapy, provided by volunteers, for foster children and their families. The pioneering program in this area was called "A Home Within", started by Toni Heinemann in San Francisco. The name of this program reflected the idea that psychotherapy could strengthen the self, a kind of "home within" for children who had been deprived of an external home from which they had been removed owing to abuse and/or neglect. Another project, originating in New York, was called, more relationally, "The Fostering Connection", emphasizing that what was to be fostered was a connection with outside people, with a therapist, and with foster and biological families. In all these programs, no one was paid monetarily; therapists were "paid" by having access to free supervision, provided by unpaid volunteer supervisors or peer supervisors. "A Home Within" had a slogan: "One Therapist, One Patient, for as long as it takes". This slogan was not adopted by the "Fostering Connection" in recognition of the fact that most patients and families did not stay for as long as the therapist might have thought it would take to repair the psychic damage done to abused and deprived children.

As noted, there had been some short-lived forays into a communitarian version of psychoanalysis in Europe, fostered by none other than Sigmund Freud himself. Outside the United States, psychoanalysis was less sharply segregated into the private sector. In England, psychoanalysis *per se* persists, albeit precariously, under the auspices of the National Health Service at the Tavistock

Institute's clinic, with boundaries between psychotherapy and psychoanalysis somewhat less sharply defined, as technical adjustments are made to accommodate migrant, economically impoverished, culturally non-mainstream patients. In parts of Scandinavia, the private, office-based practice of psychoanalysis is funded by the government, with analysts paid a salary which on an hourly basis is much lower than hourly fees in the United States. In India, Honey Oberoi Vahali, a leading member of the International Psychoanalytic Association, works with undomiciled people and Tibetan migrants in Delhi, out of the office and for no fee. In Argentina and throughout Latin America psychoanalysis is accessible to people across the socioeconomic spectrum, as fees are relatively low.

In 2020, in the months before the COVID virus was identified and studied and a vaccination developed and distributed, the office setting for psychoanalysis (and everything else) became off-limits, a site of mortal danger. For psychoanalysts and psychotherapists the frame had to be rethought with remote sessions via zoom the only option. The distinction between psychoanalysis and psychotherapy persisted in language but over time was replaced by a more salient distinction between remote and in-person settings as COVID, in the popular imagination, became a particularly virulent flu.

Meanwhile, to the extent that the very essence of psychoanalysis had been defined by its frame, the field was rocked to its core. The "community" had invaded the sacrosanct psychoanalytic setting. The recognition and therapeutic use of unconscious processes had to be retrieved and relocated in a less clearly demarcated framework, like art in the street. Community Psychoanalysis, as yet not clearly defined, entered common parlance. Analytic journals and conferences quickly took up the challenge of filling in the conceptual and technical gaps.

In response to the availability of a grant to fund a psychoanalytic project on the streets, as mentioned above, the American Psychoanalytic Association's Community Psychoanalysis working group, led by James Barron of the Boston Psychoanalytic Society and Institute, and including PINC and a number of APSA institutes, mobilized to execute a program for undomiciled people on the streets of Portland and other cities and towns of Oregon. At that point the need to develop an idea of how to think about and how to carry out some form of psychoanalysis out of the office dovetailed with the need to figure out how psychoanalysis could survive the pandemic. It was a perfect storm of factors creating tailwinds for Community Psychoanalysis, but still this version of psychoanalysis needed to be defined in theory and in practice.

The working group quickly addressed both tasks. A course was put together within weeks with a syllabus that included pioneering works in Community Psychoanalysis, placing it in the theoretical landscape, and taught remotely by many of the authors of that work from around the United States. This 12-week course was meant to be taught in psychoanalytic institutes around the country, eventually to form the core of institutional training tracks. The working group was joined by analysts who had made a strong beginning in developing tracks in Michigan by Paula Kliger, in San Francisco by Lee Slome, and in Washington-Baltimore by Lizbeth Moses. The seminar was meant to bring Community Psychoanalysis among those trained in, and practicing mainstream psychoanalysis as best they could, together with a wide spectrum of community-based clinicians. The group aimed to ensure that each class would be composed of approximately equal numbers of institute-based analysts and candidates, and community-based clinicians. Some people belonged to both categories.

The Sunday group pulled itself together on a dime because the virus wouldn't wait and people were suffering. The Sunday group was composed of people who had one or another form of clinical experience out of private offices and had access to the few journal articles that addressed such work. So what we did was this: we had a series of classes with a theme, we had an experience brainstorming on and around that theme, and then we debriefed at the end, trying to make sense out of what happened.

7 Varieties of Efforts to Link the Social with the Intrapsychic

Freud

The foundation for Community Psychoanalysis was laid by analysts, starting with Freud, who built conceptual bridges between the intrapsychic dynamics of individuals and societal dynamics. Freud (1921, 1939) blazed a trail here with his explorations of the dynamics of antisemitism, the historical roots of the Oedipus complex, religious movements, and mass psychology.

Freud begins his article on "Mass Psychology" (1921) with the following statement that recognizes the embeddedness of the individual in the community:

> The antithesis of the individual and social or mass psychology, which at first glance may seem to us very important, loses a great deal of its sharpness on close examination. Individual psychology is of course directed at the individual in isolation, tracing the ways in which he seeks to satisfy his drive impulses, but only rarely, in specific exceptions, is it able to disregard the relationships between the individual and others-----the psychology of the individual is also social psychology in this extended but wholly justified sense.
>
> (p. 17)

Freud goes on to note how the behavior of individuals in a social context is notably different than behavior in isolation, particularly with respect to disinhibition. He writes: "The mass is impulsive, inconstant, and excitable. It is guided almost exclusively by unconscious motives" (p. 25). Freud emphasizes how members of a "mass" powerfully identify with the male leader. Under the influence of a "herd instinct", individuals become powerfully suggestible. Freud further traces the origin of mass psychology to the "primal horde", led by a powerful leader who is killed by his followers acting as a group. Herein, for Freud, via Lamarckian evolution,[1] lies the origin of the Oedipus complex and the superego: the patricidal impulse in the male child and guilt. A link is thus forged between social events and intrapsychic structure but via the culture-free *deus ex machina* of inheritance of acquired characteristics.

DOI: 10.4324/9781003661146-8

Ferenczi and American Interpersonalists

Other analysts took varying approaches to integration of social dynamics with intrapsychic dynamics. Ferenczi (1933) avoided the need for Freud's Lamarckist *deus ex machina* by accounting for the Oedipus complex in intra-familial social terms. Where Freud saw the transmission of an ancient father-son scenario via Lamarckian evolution, Ferenczi (1933) saw a "confusion of tongues" between parent and child whereby affection gets sexualized. This transformation, presumably, originating in the parent, not the child, is socially, not intrapschically, transmitted. A sense of guilt in the child is produced by the child's taking on what would otherwise be the parent's guilt, via a mechanism Ferenczi called "identification with the aggressor".

Psychoanalysis in Colonial Context: Fanon and Elias

Gaztambide (2024) extends this notion to account for Frantz Fanon's (1963) understanding of colonized peoples' self-denigration in identification with their colonizers. Fanon was a psychiatrist and psychoanalyst from the Caribbean island nation of Martinique. He noted the corrosive effect of French denigration of the people of Martinique on their self-images. Thus, the social world found its way into the intrapsychic world, setting up and perpetuating a circular process of exploitation and oppression via identification with the (colonial) aggressor.

Gaztambide shows how Ferenczi thus opened up links between European psychoanalysis and the Afro-Caribbean colonial world. In a colonial context in which power imbalance was violently imposed, Fanon was led to prioritize the external world as the primary source of self-denigration and associated psychopathology following on identification with the aggressor. Also in a colonial context, Elias (1994) emphasized power as the key element in pathological internalization in colonial contexts. Thus, the path was paved which Foucault (1980) was later to follow.

His perspective led Fanon to migrate to Algeria where he joined the war to liberate that country from French rule. Eventually, he concluded that violent resistance was necessary for peoples whose internal and external worlds were thus corrupted, thereby attempting to rectify the pathology of power imbalance at its root.

Fanon's perspective was validated by the struggle of the people of Haiti to free themselves of French rule at the end of the eighteenth century. Haiti was the site of the first and only large-scale successful slave revolt in the Caribbean, indeed, the world. It would be more accurate, however, to refer to the Haitian slave revolt as partially successful since in the process of gaining freedom the former slaves were forced to borrow money from French banks to reimburse former slave owners for the loss of their source of free labor. Extreme poverty in Haiti is largely attributable to the large sums that had to be paid to the banks. The loans amounted to 90 million francs as of 1838. It took until 1947 before these loans were fully paid off.

Discussion of reparations paid to former slaves rarely, if ever, includes the fact that it was former slave owners to whom reparations were paid. In the case of Britain, it was the Government that paid reparations to former slave owners in 1833 when the slave trade was finally outlawed. This debt was finally paid off in 2015. The passive compliance of the descendents of slaves in the former French and British colonies is a testament to how deeply their subordination had psychically penetrated.

Bion, coming from a psychoanalytic background, used as a template a model of individual psychodynamics foregrounded in anxiety and defense originating in intrapsychic psychoanalytic theory. Foulkes (Foulkes & Anthony, 1957) was also a psychoanalyst, but his template gave priority to group dynamics. Dalal (2002, p. 111) puts a sharp point on the contrast by comparing Foulkes to Winnicott.

> Where Winnicott says that the clue to social and group psychology is the psychology of the individual (1958, p. 15), Foulkes would reverse the statement to say that the clue to individual psychology is to be found in the psychology of the social and the group.

In postcolonial London Fakhry Davids studied what he called "internal racism", i.e. internalized denigrating stereotypes applied to self and others on a racial basis. These originate and are perpetuated in the stereotypes and power imbalances described by Fanon, as above. Davids describes the psychic deformations originating in colonial contexts and how they can be carried forward in self-perpetuating cycles.

Bion

Bion (1987) took a different pathway to exploring the links between social and intrapsychic dynamics of groups with recourse to Kleinian concepts of anxiety and defense. Bion took for granted the omnipresence of anxiety in interpersonal relations, turning his focus to three basic defensive patterns that come to define the character of groups, as defenses constitute the character of individual people. These are dependency, fight-flight, and pairing. In the dependency pattern, group members become dependent on one group member, typically the person defined as the group leader. In the second pattern, conflict between group members defines the group, with or without some members leaving the group temporarily or permanently. In the third pattern, group members form intra-group alliances. One pair may assume the role of savior or "messiah" (Bion, 1987) in relation to the other group members. It is important to note that all three of these patterns are defined as defensive, in the sense that they distract from or undermine the purpose of the group, the assigned work which constitutes the group *raison d'etre*. Note that attachment is not noted as a basic group function: people join groups to work, or they avoid work. The possibility that there are non-work groups is bypassed by limiting the focus to work groups. One wonders, nonetheless, what might evolve in social groups in which assigned tasks are missing or marginal.

Group Analysis: Dalal: Group Analysis and the Symbolism of Skin Color

In his book *Race, Colour, and the Processes of Racialization,* Farhad Dalal gives a very useful and illuminating historical and cross-cultural overview of the evolution of meaning-making around color. Generally speaking, white or light color tends to be associated with purity, and black or dark color with dirt, sin, and evil. This color polarization is not absolute. There are black representations of the Virgin Mary in southern Spain. In the chapter entitled "The Whiteness of the Whale" in *Moby Dick* (Melville, 1929) Herman Melville writes:

> ——white is specially employed in the celebration of the Passion of our Lord; though in the Vision of St. John, white robes are given to the redeemed, and the four-and-twenty elders stand clothed in white before the great-white throne, and the Holy One that sitteth there white like wool; yet for all these accumulated associations, with whatever is sweet, and honorable, and sublime, there yet lurks an elusive something in the innermost idea of this hue, which strikes more of panic to the soul than that redness which affrights in blood. White is specially employed in the celebration of the Passion of our Lord; though in the Vision of St. John, white robes are given to the redeemed, and the four-and-twenty elders stand clothed in white before the great-white throne, and the Holy One that sitteth there white like wool
>
> (Melville, 1929)

Dalal (2002) uses the felicitous term "racialization" to indicate that human beings are "raced", acquire a "race", a position in society, via a racializing process that is essentially social. In examining this racializing process, Dalal focuses on the historical evolution of the valences of color terms applied to human skin colors, from negative to neutral to positive. He acknowledges that although "black" and "dark" sometimes have a positive valence (in the "black", indicating profitable, or "black is beautiful"), associations with darkness are overwhelmingly negative (dirty, evil). Associations with "white" tend toward the positive (clean, pure). In Sanskrit, the ancient Indian language, the word for color also is the word for caste, with darker skinned people generally of lower caste. The highest caste people, Brahmins, are assigned spiritual occupations, while people of the lowest castes are assigned work popularly considered polluting (cleaning latrines, burying the dead). Gandhi sought to turn the system on its head by volunteering to clean latrines, while Ghent (1990) pointed out that "shit", referred to as compost, is the source of life.

Fromm

Fromm (1941) proposed that the dominant socioeconomic system at a particular historical moment shaped a typical character style and constellation of defenses to produce people who best fit into the socioeconomic requirements of the time. For example, in a late capitalist context in which competitive, individualistic "marketing personalities" tend to emerge, people are organized to sell themselves like commodities. Personality development is driven by the needs to fit successfully into an economic system. Family life and parenting styles are thus shaped, primarily, by the external world rather than by internal needs and drives, rather than, or in addition to, the other way around. This picture of the interaction of the external world and individual personality fit well with the times, in which there was a sharp contrast between capitalist and socialist systems. In more recent, postcolonial times, and in the wake of slavery, psychoanalytic theories of child development, personality formation, and psychic structure have highlighted the salience of the distribution of power and privilege in society as it affects the experience of people in various social groups.

It should be noted that there is a formative historical context for how each of these factors, power and privilege, are defined. Slavery entails a sharp asymmetry in the distribution of power between slaves and slave owners, with slave owners having the ability to control almost every aspect of the lives of their slaves, from sexual behavior to economically productive work. Locus of control (Rotter, 1966) among slaves is skewed toward the external with profound psychological consequences transgenerationally for slaves and slaveowners and their descendants (Parker, 2019). Differences in locus of control shape preconceptions about groups and self-perceptions defined racially across multiple generations.

The Question of Priority Remains

Intrapsychically oriented theorists do take account of the impact of the social but restore the intrapsychic focus, maintaining the primacy of the intrapsychic via recourse to the concept of internalization. One might wonder what a theory would look like if the intrapsychic and the social were each regarded as having their own integrity but interacting in some sort of complementarity or balance. On a theoretical or abstract level, finding this sort of balance would pose a challenge, in that it would be awkward mechanically to accompany each statement that implies intrapsychic primacy, with another that balances it out with a statement to the effect that one must keep in mind the role of the social, and vice versa. But not to do so would run the risk of being quoted out of context in support of individual primacy or social primacy. In an either-or framework which is pervasive in our psychoanalytic culture, such qualifications might indeed be called for, laborious though the process might be.

What is at stake in debates about the relative primacy of intrapsychic vs. interpersonal vs. various forms of macro-social influences on psychic life? On one level, there is a question about the domain of psychoanalysis, the very identity of the field. In his day, Freud's distinctive contribution was to develop a theory of psychopathology based on the balance of purely intrapsychic psychological forces, the sexual drives and defenses. In Freud's theory other people were seen as significant primarily as objects of sexual drives. A foundational split between Freud and Ferenczi formed over the question of whether interactions between people could be pathogenic, aside from the impact of events in the interpersonal realm. For example, Ferenczi thought that betrayal, and mystification, i.e. induced confusion in children, around sexual abuse, was the primary pathogenic factor when children were molested by adults, as opposed to sexual overstimulation *per se* that exerted its pathogenic influence by overwhelming the child's paychic apparatus, i.e. his or her capacity to maintain psychic integrity. Following Ferenczi, H.S. Sullivan (1953) and others in the American interpersonal school (e.g. Fromm-Reichmann, Levenson) emphasized mystification and selective inattention, as primary pathogenic factors, not reducible to intrapsychic drive-defense conflicts or capacity to maintain psychic integrity. British object relations theorists e.g. Klein (1952) and her followers, and the Scottish analyst W.R.D. Fairbairn (1952) as well as Winnicott aimed to integrate intrapsychic and interpersonal forces in one way or another. The so-called "Middle School" initiated by Winnicottians took a middle way between the Kleinians who, relatively speaking, emphasized intrapsychic forces like the death instinct, derived from the aggressive drives, and those who emphasized the impact of the environment, in the form of its holding and containing function for young children. Greenberg and Mitchell (1983) provided a lucid summary of the state of psychoanalysis in the mid- to late-twentieth century based on relative emphasis on the internal and external worlds. Theories that emphasize the intrapsychic domain in pathogenesis are most compatible with an emphasis on the curative effect of insights via enhanced ego function, whereas theories emphasizing interpersonal pathogenesis are most compatible with curative factors related to generalization of analytic enactment resolution between patient and analyst. Theories emphasizing macro-social pathogenesis lead to ideas of cure via social change, which brings us to Erich Fromm.

Historical Context Shapes Individual/Social Prioritization in Theory: Power, Oppression, Domination

In the wake of slavery in the United States and elsewhere, a sense of guilt and responsibility remains, feeding movements for reparative social change. Theories that emphasize social influence on personality development and psychodynamics fit better with an era concerned with social change, as opposed to theories that look to inherent factors, like universal drives, as ways to understand how society has come to be the way it is. Theories that emphasize group dynamics, like that of Foulkes, fit the need, especially those that high-light dynamics around power (Elias, 1994) to understand how society came to oppress people to such an extent.

In an era of acute concern about racism, discrimination, and ethnocentrism, especially after a number of police killings of Black men in the United States and explosions of violence in the Middle East, it became increasingly apparent that one's social position strongly influences experience of events in the social sphere. For a person who grew up in an African-American ghetto, police killings of Black men came as no surprise. Black children from the ghetto are raised to be wary of the police, to avoid calling attention to themselves in the presence of the police, to avoid interactions that might grab the attention of the police.

Police killings of Black men are hardly news to many African-American people in the United States and around the world. Depressing and enraging, but not shocking. For many upper middle class White people, used to viewing police as friendly and protective, protective against *black* criminals, the news about police killings came as a wake-up call. For Black parents, well accustomed to worry about their children's run-ins with police, this was old news, as was the cluelessness of well-meaning White people about many aspects of racialized reality.

Psychoanalysts, too, have diversity in their ranks to a degree. There are Black analysts too, not many, but a few. A Black analyst might be more likely than a White analyst to respond to a White child patient's provocative behavior by seeing it as a possibly valuable occasion for limit setting, while the Black analyst may see a need to make it clear that provocative behavior around White authorities may amount to "cruising for a bruising", or worse, far worse.

So the meaning of behavior varies along with the social position of both parties to an analytic interaction. Meaning is contextual, for patients *and* analysts, and emerges from their interaction. Thus, group dynamics shape the construction of meaning in interpersonal relationships, including the transferences and countertransferences of the analytic relationship.

Note

1 Freud's invocation of Lamarckian evolution to explain the origin of supposedly innate patricidal impulses and associated guilt has the quality of a *deus ex machina*. Some, e.g. Bose, as noted above, have questioned the cross-cultural universality of this complex. Contemporary feminist theorists have also noted the universalizing of the gender categories in Freud's particular cultural context. If we don't assume, by fiat, the universality of a struggle for dominance among males, the question of the origin of such a struggle remains open, perhaps attributable to specific local cultural factors.

8 Race, Social Class, and Culture Join Gender and Sexual Orientation at the Center of Psychoanalytic Study, Adding Energy to Community Psychoanalysis in the United States

Returning to the development of the APSA seminar in Community Psychoanalysis: just as the seminar was starting, the police murder of George Floyd, on top of numerous previous killings (Eric Garner, Michael Brown, and many other Black people in the early 2020s), brought public attention to systemic and pervasive racism which had of course existed for many years in the slavery and post-slavery years, sparking the "Black Lives Matter" protests. In this context, HFI expanded, developing a subsidiary, Harlem Family Services (HFS), to provide clinical services to people of all ages in Harlem. The attention of mainstream psychoanalysis was thus drawn a bit closer to what had existed on the margins as Community Psychoanalysis, including the processes by which psychoanalysts excluded the same populations, the same groups of people who were marginalized in society at large. These marginalized groups consisted essentially of people with relatively dark skin, people with relatively low socioeconomic status (SES), defined by low income, zip code of residence, educational background, and highest degree attained. The "pure gold" form of psychoanalysis with meetings multiple times per week in a private space, with a relatively high fee was, and is, generally reserved for people of high SES. Freud (1919) had called for "free clinics", psychoanalysis for all, but this ideal did not long survive transplantation to places where free markets reigned supreme (Jacoby, 1983). It was noted by some analysts that private practice patients and analysts were overwhelmingly white and well-to-do. Community Psychoanalysis, i.e. psychoanalysis with the rest of the population, hung by a thread, supported by a few. The pandemic, and "Black Lives Matter", threw a monkey wrench into this situation.

Accordingly, for a time there has been more attention paid by analysts to race and SES within psychoanalysis. There have been papers published in journals focusing on social issues (e.g. *Psychoanalysis, Culture & Society*) as well as in more mainstream journals (e.g. *Psychoanalytic Dialogues*, and the *Journal of the American Psychoanalytic Association*). The American Psychoanalytic Association established the "Holmes Commission" led by Dorothy Holmes, a prominent African-American psychoanalyst, to study the status of race and SES in psychoanalytic training and practice.

DOI: 10.4324/9781003661146-9

Fractures Over the Place of Antisemitism

As of this writing, the Israel-Hamas war has scrambled some of these efforts, as many analysts claim that antisemitism has been neglected in the field as a major, if not *the* major, form of global prejudice. Others, focusing on post-colonial developments, see violence against Palestinians as the quintessential form oppression takes in our world. The anti-racist and anti-ethnocentric movement within psychoanalysis has been stressed to the point of fracture.

The 2024 Election and the Return of Donald Trump

As I write, it is one month since Donald Trump was elected President of the United States. It is too early to judge the impact of a second Trump administration on communitarianism and individualism in the United States or to draw any conclusions about whether recent political shifts in this regard were reflected in the election results.

Among left-leaning people in the United States it is commonplace to regard the election as reflecting an abandonment of social responsibility, as programs aiming at care for those in economic poverty, undomiciled, hungry people seem to be facing drastic cuts in government programs aimed at alleviating their deprivation and distress. Further supporting this line of thinking is the widening gap between economically rich and poor, the growing level of income inequality in the United States.

There is another line of thinking that comes to opposite conclusions. One tributary of this line of thought is that left-leaning people tend to focus on only one subgroup of economically distressed (often racially or ethnically distinct, e.g. urban black or Latino, people) while overlooking the rest (e.g. rural, White working-class people in economic distress) who, it seems, favored Trump and Vance.

The second tributary consists of concern that government support for people in economic poverty tends to disable initiative, the entrepreneurial spirit that has moved the United States economy forward.

When all sides of this debate are recognized, it becomes more difficult to look at the issues as readily polarized, easier to see the dice as loaded from the beginning by peoples' self-interest or self-esteem, e.g. sanctimony based on guilt or guilt avoidance.

Freud had claimed (1926) back in the early days of psychoanalysis that the marginal position of Jews in *fin-de-siècle* Vienna had sensitized Jews to the effect of exclusion and marginalization of other oppressed people. Jews, from Karl Marx on, had led movements for social justice and economic equality. Nonetheless, antisemitism often fed on the mythology of Jews as rich, money lenders, exploitative. In his film, *Shoah (Holocaust)* the filmmaker Claude Lanzmann asked a group of Polish Catholic women standing outside a church why the Nazis had so focused their violence on Jews. After a few minutes of hemming and hawing, in response to which Lanzmann kept refining and repeating his question, one of the women finally said "because they have all the money!"

This is not a totally surprising comment from people who have studied Holocaust history. One typical explanation might focus on the fact that Jews traditionally were not allowed to own land in Europe; money lending, banking, was one of the few remaining ways to make a living. No wonder that Polish peasants might think that Jews had all the money. Never mind that Jesus, a Jew, overturned the money changers' tables outside the Temple.

How distressing, then, that in the end, pressure from Jewish donors to withhold donations from elite universities contributed to university presidents cracking down on pro-Palestinian demonstrations.

This deep split within psychoanalysis opened up in the wake of the resurgence of interest in Community Psychoanalysis during the COVID pandemic. At the very beginning of the APSA-sponsored seminar in Community Psychoanalysis was the murder of George Floyd by police in Minnesota. The nascent seminar in Community Psychoanalysis addressed crises in the streets, and in the seminar room, in real time. The feelings and anxieties felt by group members, teachers and students, were no longer abstractions. Each class became a process group, an exercise in improvisation. The participants learned by doing. They "made the road by walking" using the phrase coined by Brazilian social activist Paolo Freire (1972).

This situation contained moving parts that in the end came together in a destructive explosion. There was a pressure cooker of Palestinian rage about the conditions of life in Gaza. There was a long-simmering fear of a new outburst of antisemitic or anti-Jewish violence on the model of the Holocaust, there was the Israeli success at courting the Arab world, enticing Saudi Arabia, Jordan, the UAE, and others into the growth potentials in linking the accumulated economic wealth of the petro-economies of the Arab world to the entrepreneurial energy of Israel and its Euro-American allies. Who might feel left out of this potential new world order, and who might object to it in principle? This question was just beginning to be considered, when Hamas took explosive and deadly action to torpedo it before it really got off the ground.

Israel had been on the verge of making an economic and political home for itself in the Middle East, except they forgot about a couple of million Gazans who already felt forgotten about by their Arab kinspeople. By viciously attacking Israel and Israelis on October 7, 2024, Hamas lit the fuse on pan-Arab hostility to Israel by provoking Israel to threaten to annihilate Gaza with all its Arab inhabitants. In defense of its right to exist, Israel took actions eliciting widespread horror and disapproval. Israel's widely publicized (except within Israel) violence against Palestinian civilians in Gaza, for some far overshadowed in the public consciousness the atrocities committed against Israeli civilians by Hamas operatives. The killing of Palestinians by megaton bombs and the laying waste of hospitals, neighborhoods, and whole cities overshadowed the narratives of having been raped, having their children killed in front of them, of individual Israeli women. Hamas succeeded in many quarters in portraying their side as innocent victims, the Israeli side as well-funded and well-armed perpetrators. For others, the ancient, but perpetually contemporary, narrative of Jews as victims was infused with new energy, electrifying a rightward shift in US politics. Finally, Donald Trump's Republican Party swept into power in the 2024 elections.

The Arab-Jewish Israeli conflict took on a fine point when the scenario was enacted on US university campuses. Reflecting the unequal distribution of wealth in US society, many of the largest donors to the most prominent universities were Jewish. These alumni exerted outsize influence on the institutions that had become dependent on their money. Palestinians and other "Third World" students and alumni had moral authority; their presence reflected a societal impulse toward reparation for prior exclusionary actions. This social justice perspective had previously been identified with people "of color" and their allies who were often Jewish. With a long history of having been victimized, Jewish sympathies were frequently with oppressed people, as reflected in the Passover narrative. For some time, the alliances between Jews and people "of color" were under stress as Jews were frequently among the privileged in ghettos, the landlords, store owners, and such. Now that financial muscles were being flexed in defense of the new status quo which for some time had begun to favor Jews, the old hierarchies were reinstated and reinforced.

In the end, the situation is composed of two traumatized peoples who keep retraumatizing each other. Trying to live in the same narrow band of cultivable land, studded with places that are holy to one or the other group, or to both, and with a long, long history of deadly conflict, it seems unrealistic to expect that they can coexist peacefully. Third parties that seem in a position to mediate can try to intervene, if they can get along. Perhaps the economic interests of third parties like the United States and the European Union on one side and the Gulf Arab states on the other can make for a viable, if fragile, detente. Of course, Russia, China, Iran, etc., must buy in——.

. This might be a good time to emphasize that in this section I am speaking of these groups in generalities. Jews, people of color, Arabs, and other groups were and are composed of multiple subgroups divided by intersections of gender, social class, age, and other factors. Even as Jews rose to prominence among the newly resurgent US right wing, the great majority of US Jews voted for Kamala Harris in 2024. Then there are the individual constellations that can never quite be reduced to one or more of these factors.

Ironically, but predictably, the concentration of economic wealth and political power in the United States and elsewhere is being accomplished by democratic means. A system of free and fair elections in the United States meant originally to give everyone a voice spoke, in 2024, in favor of a system that all at once shut down or greatly diminished efforts at looking after the economic and political well-being of a wide swath of the population. *In media res*, several factors and forces, long overlooked by many people who had a comfortable position in the *ancien regime*, seem to have been in play. Those of us who find psychoanalysis a useful tool in thinking about large-scale social movements might be grimly gratified to find that this way of thinking illuminates the processes that, for long, have been eating away at the foundations of our field.

If psychoanalysis is devoted to uncovering marginalized forces and people, we should not be surprised to stumble upon what many of us in the field have overlooked. The clinically critical phenomenon of enactment should put us on the alert to the likelihood that when we set out to address a problem, the first thing that happens is that we, the would-be problem-solvers, reproduce that problem among ourselves. Our would-be ameliorative work, to our horror, seems to end up exacerbating the problem we were trying to solve. That is what the phenomenon of transference teaches us. As Freud taught us, we cannot conquer an enemy *in absentia* or *in effigie*.

The problem at hand is that of marginalization, of overlooking things. So, of course, we start out by overlooking things. Not only this gives us an opportunity to despair, to give up, but it also gives us an opportunity to find a way out through surrender (as Ghent taught us). Which marginalized people have we, the erstwhile elite of psychoanalysis, been overlooking?

An interpretation was provided in 2016 by J.D. Vance with his book *Hillbilly Elegy*.

9 Psychoanalytic Ideals of Individualism, Objectivity, and Subjectivity
Can They All Coexist?

The eighteenth- and nineteenth-century scientific ideal of objectivity is conducive to individualism. Insofar as objectivity entails a split between the observer and the observed, each must be sharply separated from the other. The observed is alone on the couch, the observer is out of sight behind the couch.

Objectivity is obviously at the core of conventional psychoanalysis (there is, after all, only one patient on the couch, with a diagnosis that is not shared with anyone else) and it is less obviously but at least equally deeply embedded in almost everyone's thinking, at least in middle class, white, North American culture. Since the "observed" is a human being with a subjectivity, capable of observing the analyst/observer, albeit out of sight, we need a less sharp split, a less uncompromising individualism for psychoanalysis. In this culture, our ways of thinking are implanted so deeply that it just doesn't occur to most of us to try to uproot them. At the same time, paradoxically, our lived experience includes very powerful identifications with groups and blurry boundaries between each of us and others. Day to day, we go on juggling these contradictions and paradoxes.

Here is the point where the boundary between individual psychology and communal psychology becomes indeterminate. Individual psychoanalysis posits processes of internalization and "communities" of internal objects, or "internal communities" to take account of what is left out when we try to draw a hard and fast line around the physical individual, defined by the skin. Here too there are complications. Physiological processes (e.g. blood pressure, gastrointestinal processes, etc.) have been shown to be responsive to what happens outside the skin boundary. Psychoanalysts, in desperation to isolate the physical individual, have placed the patient inside the boundary wall, sound proofed, sometimes even with double doors and elaborate systems for outsiders to announce themselves and to gain entrance!

Even with the dyad's boundaries firmly reinforced so as to permit, in theory, uncontaminated study of the physically and mentally defined "patient" and with outsiders defined as internalized objects, there is another problem: the analyst himself or herself *also* contains internalized objects, communities of them! Policing these intruders are border patrol officers put in place by the training analysis.

DOI: 10.4324/9781003661146-10

Can Individualism Coexist with Communalism?

Reflecting on the function of the training analysis can illuminate the perceived or desired function of psychoanalysis in general. In the language of ego psychology, "where id was, there ego shall be" (Freud, 1933). But in the language of object relations a la Fairbairn (1952), the goal is to extend the dominion of the "central ego" in relation to those versions of the ego infused with sexual and/or aggressive drives: in Fairbairn's language: libidinal ego, anti-libidinal ego. Switching to Kleinian language, the goal is to extend and fortify the operation of the depressive position which, with its integrative function, refers (switching back to ego psychological language for the moment) to something like "the synthetic function" of the ego (Nunberg, 1932).

This last statement is inexact in a number of ways, but the point is that in acknowledging that the training analysis is intended to fortify and extend the dominion of the ego, the observing function of the ego, the agenda of psychoanalysis is clarified. This agenda can be stated inexactly in the language of various versions of psychoanalysis in relation to other mental agencies, whether conceived as id and superego, or as internal objects, or in some other terms. I say "inexactly" because each of the psychoanalytic languages carries with it baggage that is in some ways continuous with the rest of psychoanalysis and in some ways radically different (see Greenberg & Mitchell, 1983, for an extensive explanation on this point).

As the field has splintered into various schools each of which carries a loyalty to one or another psychoanalytic language and way of thinking, the potential for moving ahead in an integrative fashion has largely been left by the wayside. I suggest that bringing an individualistic perspective together with a collectivistic focus has great integrative potential in psychoanalysis. The time is right: from the margins, the socioeconomic and political worlds have been claiming a place at the center, even among historically individualistic schools of psychoanalysis.

Paradox

How to move ahead with an integration? First, note there is a strand in psychoanalytic theory that tends toward paradoxical thinking, often with roots in India. Theorists pursuing this path avoid either-or splits, like Bose who as we noted earlier tried to nudge Freud away from gender splits. In British psychoanalysis Winnicott and Klein introduced paradoxical thinking in the form of transitional space (Winnicott, 1971) and the depressive position (Klein, 1952) which paradoxically made room for coexistence of love and destruction. Ghent (1990) put paradox center stage in his paper *Paradox and Process*. From Bose's overture to Freud, and onward, then, there is a firm foundation in psychoanalysis for a paradoxical coexistence of individualism and communalism, such that there is no contradiction in finding a place for Community Psychoanalysis.

Kleinian theory is a thoroughly non-dualistic theory, based on paradox and coexistence of seeming opposites. As emphasized by Ogden (1986), by basing her developmental schema on positions, rather than stages, Klein makes it possible to conceive of coexistence of paranoid-schizoid (ps) and depressive (d) positions just as the depressive position is characterized by coexistence of good and bad. In a stage theory, based on a developmental hierarchy, the earlier stage is supplanted by the later stage. This builds in an either-or feature, easily mappable onto a maturity distinction.

The distinction between "paranoid-schizoid" and "depressive" in itself is not inconsistent with an either-or structure. What is truly distinctive about the Kleinian theoretical structure is that the paranoid-schizoid position has its own value. Without ps, in the Kleinian set up, d, as they call the depressive position, gets people bogged down in indecision.

We need "ps" and we need "d", in some sort of fluid adaptable balance with each other. Polarizing ps and d paralyzes us or gets us into trouble by disabling reflective functioning. If we polarize ps and d, each loses its distinctive psychic value, just as masculinity and femininity lose their distinctive psychic place that made Girindrasekhar Bose's argument to Freud, and nonbinary gender theory, complementary. It is also the piece that, beyond expanding the locations in which psychoanalysis can be conducted, opens up the field, making it more compelling and inclusive.

How do these very abstract theoretical points play out "on the ground?" In actual sessions, with particular patients? Are there noticeable differences when one stops polarizing individualism and collectivism? The answer is: in some ways, there is no difference at all. In some ways, everything is different. A comparable question might be: how does a nonbinary approach to gender manifest in actual interactions, in actual relationships?

Peoples' behavior is not necessarily affected by their ideologies or abstract theoretical commitment and predilections. From this point of view, theory affects what people *think* they should be doing, or how they *judge* what they do, post hoc. In that sense, changes on a theoretical level may not change what they do very much, but it may change how they feel about what they do. People are generally not very aware of much of what they do, in the therapy office, or standing at a bar. When therapists see and hear themselves in sessions on videotape, they are often surprised by what they observe. If they change in the direction of being less judgmental of their behavior, they may not change what they do very much but they may feel more free, responsible, and centered and all that may make a lot of difference. This sense of autonomy is related to one's actions, but not only that: one feels more self-actualizing in one's experience, in the way one deals with conflict, in the process that *eventuates* in action. Sartre (1993) and other existentialists emphasized that ultimately one's self is defined by one's actions and by one's choices. I think he underemphasized how one's self emerges as well in the process and experience that underlie and overlay action *per se*.

One's self-experience emerges, inevitably, in a social matrix, even when one's behavior is definable as self-centered or narcissistic. There is no one-to-one correlation between the way we think and the way we behave. Some people make a point of not letting their impact on others divert them from self-centered life choices. There is a large body of anecdotal work (Shaw, 2013) emerging in recent years from people whose lives have been impacted by "malignant narcissists", spouses, children, co-workers, and so on. These are people who've made a point of *not* paying attention to how they impact others; reading these books impresses one with the huge impact their inattention has had on others. These people may be collectivists on an intellectual basis but narcissistic in their behavior and impact on others. We are all, perhaps unwitting collectivists even in our resolute self-centeredness.

This last point illustrates how individualism and collectivism are literally inseparable. The culture of narcissism described by Lasch (1979) in his book is literally a collective phenomenon. Members of a highly individualistic culture compose a herd of individualistic people! The impact of so-called "traumatic narcissists" (Shaw, 2013) has a huge effect on their social/collective surround. It cannot be denied that there are conceptual distinctions to be made between individualism and collectivism. What matters to us as therapists and analysts is how these commitments affect how we think and behave in sessions, our technique. In the end we cannot ignore the impact of our technique and way of thinking on our patients, and vice versa.

If we commit ourselves to thinking and working in nonbinary fashion, how does that look? Here the analyst's subjective experience takes center stage.

Suppose the patient texts me ten minutes before the session is due to begin saying that he was delayed leaving work. Can we go overtime? Does it matter that the patient is habitually a little late? Do we need to know why he was late leaving work? Does the analyst believe, in general, that going overtime amounts to creating an unanalyzable complication? Does the analyst believe that refusing to go overtime also creates (might create? Risks creating?) an unanalyzable complication? (What does "unanalyzable" mean?) Will going overtime entail, for the analyst, losing time with family? At the gym? etc.

There are a number of possible binary-based approaches to such a situation. One would rely on strict adherence to a fixed idea of the frame. For example, with the idea that the timing of the session is a fixed aspect of the analytic frame and viewing the patient's request for extra time as a test of the analyst's resolve, the analyst could simply refuse to allow for extra time or even to answer the question (adhering to another aspect of a traditional frame).

On the other hand, contemporary interpersonal/relational analysts would likely reject such an approach, based on the claim that anonymity and neutrality are unachievable, that no matter how the analyst responds, his or her action exposes something about the analyst, to which the patient will react or will respond with their own action.

From this point of view, the analytic frame, or stance, does not prescribe particular actions, or restraint from particular actions, except generally agreed-upon unethical actions. The analytic frame becomes an approach based on the tracking of the flow of emotion and meaning-making between analyst and patient. Such reflection, tracking, is itself action, the impact of which is itself to be tracked.

Hoffman (1998), without theoretical fanfare, captured the seemingly paradoxical intertwining (inter-twin-ing) of self and other when he defined transference as the patient' experience of the countertransference (and, of course, vice versa).

Does the Standard Office Setting Influence the Patient? The Analyst?

A core premise of the office-based model in psychoanalysis is that an office context can be designed so as not to significantly disrupt the neutrality and anonymity for which the classical analyst strives. As a candidate I had as I remember, a teacher. This particular analyst had nothing hanging from the walls and wore the same blue suit to every class meeting. His office was in his residential apartment, the private section of which we candidates never got a glimpse. In contrast to some of our teachers, he never came out of his private section until the precise moment when the class was scheduled to begin.

Granted, as I write about this teacher I am aware that I am caricaturing him to fit the point I am trying to make. There is truth to the caricature I have constructed, but I am also aware of leaving out certain elements that do not fit. So I too am exposed in this effort at "objective" description with an ulterior motive. In revealing my reflections about what I have written, I expose another facet of myself, though of course also with other ulterior motives. The fundamental point is that I believe we are *always* exposing ourselves, there is no place to hide, including within the so-called office setting. In an office, we can think we have more control over what we reveal than we do when we step out into the street, into the "community", but perhaps control is the point, as Freud acknowledged when he said he preferred the patient to lie on the couch because he couldn't bear to be looked at all day (ref).

In making efforts at anonymity a *sine qua non* of the analytic stance, we train our candidates to chase a holy grail, one that is, in principle, impossible to achieve. This situation brings to mind Mitchell's (1988) reference to Stravinsky's response to a musician's complaint that one of his compositions was impossible to play. To this, Stravinsky allegedly replied: "what I am after is the sound of someone *trying* to play it".

Leaving aside for the moment the impossible question of how we (or Stravinsky) could prefer one "failed" effort over another, we can address a different question: what basis might we have for preferring one holy grail over another.

Suppose, while taking for granted that *every* analytic response exposes some aspect or aspects of the analyst's subjectivity, that our goal is to track the interplay of subjectivities. This goal underlies Hoffman's comment (1983) to the effect that transference is the patient's experience of the countertransference. This hall of mirrors takes us back to the unavoidable question of the basis on which Stravinsky might prefer one effort to play his composition over another. If we smuggle in some notion of objectivity to this effort, the holy grail becomes more tantalizing and slippery. But if we redefine the whole enterprise as aimed at learning about musicians as they try to play Stravinsky, we have shifted the focus from goal to process.

Shifting the focus in this way has significant implications, with advantages and disadvantages, for how we think about and practice psychoanalysis. If we think about psychoanalysis as the "impossible profession" on the Stravinsky model and if we train candidates to try to generate effective interventions, making judgments in this respect on objective bases, we are building in a high level of feelings of frustration and failure into psychoanalytic work. This situation is quite unstable: few people, analysts or non-analysts, are likely to be able to live with this kind of tension on an ongoing basis. Typical defenses to which analysts may turn account for what I consider to be seriously problematic aspects of psychoanalytic training and clinical work.

Given the unrealistic expectations for objectivity that I am outlining as a typical feature of the psychoanalytic model we have inherited, candidates are often led to internalize feelings of failure in a vicious circle with their supervisors and teachers. Senior analysts who train candidates and junior analysts are themselves subject to feelings of frustration and failure on the same basis. Giving critical feedback to supervisees can easily acquire a judgmental edge that displaces self-judgment into the trainee, producing and perpetuating the notorious and inhibiting "psychoanalytic superego". Trainees often learn to "play it safe", both in the treatment room and in supervision, heightening the stereotypical withholding analytic stance from which many patients and prospective patients recoil.

From this point of view, the analytic frame, or stance, does not prescribe particular actions, or restraint from particular actions, except generally agreed-upon unethical actions. The analytic frame becomes an approach based on the tracking of the flow of emotion and meaning-making between analyst and patient. Such reflection, tracking, is itself action, the impact of which is itself to be tracked.

In the end, then, psychoanalysis is a process of self-reflection, but self-reflection in the presence of an other, a specific other. This other, the analyst, has two major functions: one is to guide the patient through the process of self-reflection, what to notice, ways of thinking about what is noticed. In this, the analyst is guided by theory and tradition with respect to how to proceed. The analyst is not infallible but has the benefit of decades spent thoughtfully practicing a way of self-observation.

The other major function of the analyst is to use his or her own experience with the patient to learn about the patient. Immersed in his or her own subjectivity the analyst is doubly fallible, as his or her experience is refracted through a personal lens, but also deeply sensitive and insightful. Kleinian analysts have used the notion of "projective identification" to work with this question of the relationship between the patient's subjective experience and the analyst's. Kleinian analysts have focused on how the analyst's experience can be shaped by the patient's experience, less focused on how the patient's experience can be shaped by the analyst's. This latter perspective follows from a relational point of view which emphasizes *mutual* influence between patient and analyst. Classical perspectives, Freudian or Kleinian, to the extent that the analyst is seen as neutral and anonymous, aim, ideally, to reduce the analyst's influence on the patient to zero. Here is where there is a sharp and revealing contrast between the two approaches to psychoanalysis. As mentioned above, relational/interpersonal analysts see the analyst's effort to reduce his or her influence both as an impossible quest *and* as influencing the patient profoundly precisely because that influence is denied.

Thirdness

The shift toward a more intersubjective stance across schools of psychoanalysis is a step in the right direction. This shift has a number of manifestations: case reports reflecting to a greater degree the subjectivity and emotionality of the analyst and the interplay with the subjectivity and emotionality of the patient. Especially helpful are published reports of senior analysts recounting more openly their personal experience with patients and, especially, their learning curve with respect to finding how exploration of this experience can feed a productive analytic process. Senior and admired analysts can thus serve as role models for a new generation with respect to developing a new, more realistic, model for an intersubjective analytic stance and how to put it into practice. Exemplary here is the work of Thomas Ogden (1994) with his self-exploration in the context of what he calls the "intersubjective analytic third" and Jessica Benjamin (2004) with her personally open study of impasses in analytic work and her way of discovering ways out of impasses by expanding her focus to include the intersubjective, third space. Benjamin's work is especially helpful in that it can expand to include the socio-political world with its seemingly irresolvable impasses and efforts at resolution. The structure of dyads lends itself to both either-or polarization and enmeshment. The addition of a third term (represented by the father in some versions of Kleinian theory (1952) and the "phallus" in Lacanian theory (1978) both address the need to represent a way out from enmeshment in a dyadic context. Ogden and Benjamin add the other tack, focusing on how the addition of a third term expands an all-important space for perspective-taking in the context of self-reinforcing polarization (like Benjamin's Hegelian doer-done to structure). Both these theorists take a further step, noting how the self-reflective function, which psychoanalysis cultivates, potentially creates a third space within an individual. This theoretical move builds a bridge to the traditional dyadic psychoanalytic structure (Britton, 1992). Community Psychoanalysis, placing the dyad in the context of various forms of community, likewise adds a third term in various forms (Altman, 2010).

This particular version of the third, as it happens, adds the entire social world on small and large scales to the psychoanalytic field. Within the dyad, similarities and differences with respect to race, ethnicity, social class, gender, sexual orientation, and more, including the analyst's location on all these dimensions, are all potentially impactful, requiring attention and psychoanalytic thought. The intersubjective matrix is widened and enriched, expanding to include all these factors formerly excluded from the psychoanalytic field, which had thereby rendered the field exclusionary. In short, focusing on thirdness widens the aperture on the psychoanalytic lens, adding dimensionality to adjacent fields of study. Progress is made on resolution of impasses and dead ends on many levels, from vicious circles on a dyadic level to short-sightedness with respect to a number of other social and political levels.

It bears noting that analysts who write about the "third" tend to focus on only one aspect of thirdness: Ogden (1994) on intrapsychic access to thirdness through reverie (cf Bion) Benjamin on resolution of dyadic impasses (cf Hegel, 1807), on the opening of triadic space generated in Oedipal space, and Altman (2010) on the thirdness generated when attention is paid to socio-cultural context. It seems that foci generated in an intrapsychic or interpersonal theory persist through the transition to a "three-person" space, as it were, with few if any analysts noting that adding a third term transforms *all* psychoanalytic theories. Further, the reverse might be noted that interpersonal and intrapsychic theories are also transformed when viewed through a one-person lens. Are we not capable of binocular vision? Our brains seem to have figured out that optic nerves crossing over to the other side of the brain facilitate integration by mixing and sorting out input from the left eye and right eye. Can we envision trinocular vision (with the third eye of Hindu mythology, capable of inner, spiritual, perception)? Or uninocular vision? What would happen if we had three eyes, or only one, like the Cyclops of Greek mythology?

Adding a third space is like adding a third (or any number of) dimensions to our conception of physical space. Our bodies operate in three-dimensional space. Adding a fourth dimension (time) requires us to transcend our everyday notions of time and space, such that we must refer to the fourth dimension as space/time. Yet this adjustment is necessary in order to make sense of the documented fact that clocks run slower when the clock's velocity increases with reference to an observer/time keeper. This time differential is not a mere artifact. The human (or any) body ages faster if it moves faster than an observer who is moving relatively slower.

Theoretically speaking, one can conceive of more than four dimensions, but x-dimensional space, where x>4, cannot be described, or thought about, with reference to ordinary human experience. The language of mathematics is necessary and beyond the scope of this book.

In sum, psychoanalytic space is experientially multi-dimensional. With reference to intrapsychic "space" and interpersonal "space", there are "third" spaces where these overlap and interact, inflected by such forces and factors such as race, social class, shared and internalized cultural values, and many others. Third spaces are useful in promoting reflection and perspective-taking of the sort that facilitates breaking out of misunderstandings and impasses. The level of complexity generated by multi-dimensional third spaces is such that we must resort to nonlinear dynamic systems theory, discussed below, to begin to get a handle on how analyst and patient, buffeted about by multiple currents and cross currents, find a way to stay afloat.

Language/Words as Highly Consequential Third Term

Over 200 years ago, William Wordswoth (1802) wrote "the child is the father of the man". In so saying Wordsworth metaphorically transcended the standard, literal, meanings of all three substantive words in the stanza, rearranging them so as to create a new thought with old words. Words have literal and metaphorical meanings; words can set thought and experience in motion, ending up in unexpected, far-flung destinations. Wordsworth's words, slightly altered, ended up emerging from Sigmund Freud's pen, pointing the way toward a weight-bearing pillar of the edifice of psychoanalysis. In a different context, Jesus said: "—-anyone who will not receive the kingdom of God like a little child will never enter it" (Luke 18:17). We are all shaped by language, but we are not necessarily imprisoned by language if we know how to use words to free ourselves.

Sometimes words set up traps, confining meaning by seeming to set up polarities that strongly force our thoughts into predetermined meanings. Racial categories organized into polarized terms, i.e. black and white, exert a strong pull on our experience of what race *is* and how it organizes human relationships. It is easy to see that human skin colors are not so polarized into black and white. This perception evidently is not as influential on our experience of humanity as the categories available to us in language. Words are the tools of thought. If, to a hammer, everything is a nail, to a speaker of the English language, people are either black or white. It is possible to think outside these constraints, but it takes effort and ingenuity, even though the rich variety of people's appearance is so obvious. We say "people of color" when we know there is no such thing as people of no color.

Human thinking is commonly organized by polarities which form the bases of stereotypes. When stereotypes fail to conform to reality, the evidence of one's senses or other forms of experience, the need to organize or simplify reality tends to take precedence over fidelity to objective reality. For example, human skin color is rarely purely black or white. Skin color tends to fall in the pink-brown range. We know this, yet we continue to categorize many people as black or white. The need to polarize in the service of constructing a clear hierarchy of dominance and submission, superiority and inferiority, takes precedence, but it builds on a general cognitive predilection to prioritize clarity.

In the real, social world, on the individual and the group, e.g. political, level, behavior only roughly, if at all, conforms to stereotypical patterns. For example, there is a clarity to polarized ideologies, e.g. capitalism vs socialism. For that reason, politicians are perennially prone to oversimplifying the relationship between categories in the interest of persuading people to make choices based on stereotypes rather than grappling with the complexities of real-life choices. A countervailing tendency that may moderate extremism also commonly arises. The result is to blunt, to a degree, programs that come to seem extremist. The tripartite structure of the US government seems explicitly designed to encourage compromise and negotiation, as opposed to extremism and purity. Thus, whereas the prevalence of two political parties pulls for polarization, in the end when one party captures one governing structure (say, the presidency), the other party tends to capture another, countervailing structure, e.g. the legislative branch, which itself has two branches which must cooperate in order to exert the power of either one. Whereas purity of vision tends to arise in presidential elections organized by two political parties, the "down ballot" elections often enough mess up the picture. Here is an example of how individualism and collectivism seem destined to interact or can be designed to interact. Each individual in the voting booth must vote for only one of two (more or less) polarized candidates for President. But in the collective these same voters seem somehow magically activated to include the other side.

A parliamentary system is more messy, but to the same end. Individual voters select a collection of individuals who must, in the process of getting along well enough with each other to govern together, bridge gaps, negotiate, and compromise. In both systems ("parliamentary" and "US" or whatever you want to call it) it is the system itself that pulls millions of autonomous individuals together into a unified voice that is inclusive of complexity and contradiction. Systems theory demonstrates how something similar happens in families in which "autonomous" individuals of varying ages, developmental positions, and genders, contextualized in different peer groups with varying peer-derived cultures, etc., are somehow magically pulled together into a unified family.

Socialist initiatives tend to try to put a damper on individual initiative in efforts to encourage equitable distribution of its fruits (ignoring evidence of innovative social justice-inspired programs designed to reduce economic inequality); capitalists ruthlessly encourage individual initiative with more or less after-thought-type remedial attention paid to the consequences for those who fall by the wayside in one way or another.

Evolution in Theory: No Wonder Psychoanalysis Is Preoccupied with Conflict

In Freud's day, the individual was portrayed as caught between sexual impulses and prohibitions. That, it turned out, was the tip of an iceberg of conflict. In *Civilization and Its Discontents* (Freud, 2002) as interpreted by Bersani (2002) the individual is caught in an impossible bind: between sexual impulses and societal prohibitions. In Bersani's reading, the aggression that feeds the prohibitions gets turned on the self, creating a sadistic superego and feeding the sexual impulses in a destructive cycle.

From this point of view, failure to address community needs with psychoanalytic methods can be seen as reflecting a destructive/negating element in the attitude toward society. In Freud's schema, there is a way out: the ego functions to mediate such id-superego conflicts. There is another way out, to which I now turn. The self-organizing tendency in nonlinear dynamic systems.

10 Nonlinear Dynamic Systems

Some seemingly random collections of elements, under certain conditions, have a way of self-organizing, like eddies emerging in a rushing river (see above, and in Glick, 2011). The overall thrust of this book is to demonstrate how "Community Psychoanalysis" can emerge from a collection of individualistic and relational pieces.

The Self and the Dyad as a Nonlinear Dynamic System

So far we've been considering the self, from an objective point of view, as manifest within interactions with other people. When two or more people/selves meet and engage, the evolving interactive process brings to the fore multiple potential shapes and functions in each person/self. Each person's engagement with the other evokes one or more of the shapes that exist in the other person's repertoire. This in turn feeds back into the first person's response. A flow is set in motion, a nonlinear dynamic system. Such systems with their recurrent iterations of feedback and re-forming have characteristics common to all nonlinear dynamic systems. Now, using the language of nonlinear dynamic systems theory, one of these characteristics consists of emergent "strange attractors", i.e. patterns with a fractal structure (meaning that any element replicates the whole) that tend toward stability or recurrence, like whirlpools in a mountain stream, flowing over a series of rocks of varying sizes and shapes. Whirlpools form, each an emergent strange attractor.

I suggest that "selves", i.e. emergent and relatively stable patterns toward which complex systems tend to evolve, are likewise strange attractors. Again, their "fractal" structure refers to the fact that the structure of the whole is reproduced in each part, no matter how large or small. Some of my early supervisors used to claim that if you told them how a session started, they could tell you how the whole session would unfold. They were, in effect, claiming that a session is a fractal. A head of broccoli is a fractal. Check it out.

The "emergent" nature of strange attractors means that there is no organizer, no organizing intelligence, and no architect. Their structure spontaneously emerges. In retrospect, we can see that the potential for a particular structure

DOI: 10.4324/9781003661146-11

was always there, but prospectively we cannot foresee where a strange attractor will occur, nor precisely what shape it will take, or, in other words, what shape will emerge. Ordinary notions of cause and effect do not work; that's why we refer to these systems as "nonlinear". If there is a "God" he, she, or it is contained within the "emergent" process. That's why we refer to God as unknowable.

Harris (2005) building on the work of Esther Thelen (Thelen & Smith, 1994) has reconsidered the process of human development as a nonlinear dynamic one. Selves emerge in interpersonal interaction. These interactions, as a unit of analysis, are themselves nonlinear dynamic systems. There is something intriguing about positing a self-organizing principle to account for spontaneously arising organizations, even our very selves. This idea is unsettling to those of us who were raised on standard linear cause and effect thinking. Yet, there is too much in the universe that seemingly cannot be accounted for any other way.

Individuals Form Systems; Individuals *Are* Systems

So far we've been considering the self, from an objective point of view, as manifest within interactions with other people. When two or more people/ selves meet and engage, the evolving interactive process exposes multiple potential shapes and functions in each person/self. Each person's engagement with the other evokes one or more of the shapes that exist in the other person's repertoire. This in turn feeds back into the first person's response. A flow is set in motion, a nonlinear dynamic system. A community is a nonlinear dynamic system. No individual is an isolate, any more than an individual gnat in a swarm is disconnected from the swarm as a whole. If you try to disrupt a swarm of gnats, the swarm, or any part of it, will immediately re-form in an identical pattern. How does each individual know what to do?

When human beings are the individual elements in a system, we know from Fanon and other theorists in the object relations tradition that the system, composed of individuals, is internalized, becoming part of the inner world of each individual. Internal objects form organizations with systemic properties, as do external objects.

Imagination

Donnel Stern (1997) entitled one of his books *Unformulated Experience: From Dissociation to Imagination in Psychoanalysis,* referring to his conception of the trajectory of the analytic journey. It is easy to see how dissociation could be conceived of as a starting point, but how is "imagination" conceived as an end point, as a goal?

Laing (Laing & Esterson, 1970) once commented that psychopathology can be understood as a failure of imagination, a failure that entraps the individual in current ways of being. From this point of view, change, including therapeutic change, is inconceivable without imagination, without the capacity to imagine a new state of affairs.

Esprey (2017) added another dimension to the role of imagination in describing an initially misfired engagement with a South African patient called Thabi.

Espry tracks the evolution in her capacity to "think" (Bion, 1988), i.e. to remain mindful, in the face of racial issues in analysis as a White woman working with Black patients in apartheid South Africa. At the beginning of a ten-year period, she describes herself colluding with a "colored", i.e. South Asian, Indian, man whom she calls Denesh, by failing to engage his comment about envying White boys. Espry responded "limply" that she, too, was white. Denesh says that she is "a different kind of white", as they together move on "without further reflection", in effect, to join him in "disavowal of blackness".

Ten years later, having engaged in an extended process of self-examination, Espry is in a very different state of consciousness with respect to the dynamics of her racial(ized) self. She is much better equipped to join her Black patients in examining their race-related traumas.

After some time, there occurred the following interaction: "Talking about his childhood", Thabi, "without affect" (p. 30) said he had few childhood memories, except that he remembered his mother covering his face to protect him from daily explosions of tear gas in the township where he "grew up". Esprey recalled the fear and anxiety she herself had felt watching townships burn on television at the time. Overwhelmed by the power of what had been evoked in her, she "unimaginatively" commented that Thabi grew up in a "traumatic and frightening" environment. Thabi replied that it was no more traumatic or frightening than for any other Black person at the time.

This interaction at first felt like a dead end, until Esprey was able to note and comment on the "brief spurt of anger" in Thabi's response to her comment:

Thabi entered the next session with rich associations about interacting with a group of White people, allowing Esprey to connect with what she imagined were his feelings of being "misunderstood and judged by her". He then went on to describe the discomfort he had recently felt in an encounter group focusing on cross-racial interactions in which he was the sole Black participant. Thabi's discomfort was associated with the vicarious shame he felt being witness to White people coming to terms with their psychic blockages around race in post-apartheid South Africa. As a reader, it struck me that Thabi might well have been indicating that he felt shame identifying with Espry's awkwardness, as a White person, in responding to the "trauma" he had experienced at the hands of White people under apartheid. Perhaps he was feeling shame in identification both with Espry and with the White people in the encounter group. Disorganized by his shame, Espry could not think clearly or in resonance with Thabi. She could only make a superficial supposition about Thabi's feelings which, as he observed, "any" Black person would have felt. "Unimaginative" then meant that she lacked, for the moment, at least, the capacity to penetrate to the depths and uniqueness of

Thabi's experience, a form of loving attentiveness that goes beyond generic stereotypes.

In a sense, imagination is necessary for "true self" (Winnicott, 1960/1965) living. Winnicott speaks of "true self" as process, a flow, emergent. False self is a structure, something given, external, requiring a molding of the self to fit. Imagination is at the core of the creation of something that didn't exist before. This way of thinking gets close to the way Donnel Stern (1997) thinks about imagination when he writes:

> Who Is it that speaks from the heart? Whose language is creative language? Who is it that imagines? Is it consciousness itself? It must be. But it can't be, at least it can't be consciousness alone, because what we say at such times is beyond our power to predict. Is imagination, then, the sudden appearance of that unconscious organizing activity that I have been discussing?
>
> (1997, p. 99)

The organizing activity to which Stern refers here is the process by which experience gets formulated, made thinkable. Study of the arts, story-telling, visual arts, and so on, the whole realm of the arts, is indeed the quintessential fount of psychoanalytic creativity.

Imagination is also what makes cross-cultural understanding and communication possible. Cultural worlds of meaning, interconnecting webs of meaning, all interactions across cultural differences, require imaginative placement of oneself evoked in one's own cultural context, into another person's meaning-web. Personal meaning-making systems likewise are webs of meaning, sometimes personally idiosyncratic, sometimes locally shared, sometimes widely shared on a national or international scale. What Winnicott called "true self" is idiosyncratic, but containing elements that are widely enough shared to allow for ready communication.

As Mitchell (1993) indicated, the ethos of psychoanalysis has shifted since Freud's day. Trained as a medical doctor, Freud's concerns revolved around symptoms and cure. The underlying value system was based, as he put it, according to Jones (1953), on the ability to love and to work. But the meaning of loving and working has since evolved and changed. Freud himself was responsible for fundamental changes in the way "love" was understood, while, recently, technological change has driven changes in the way "work" is understood.

Freud (1905) was intent on developing a thorough-going theory based on drive. Thus, it was his premise that all psychic phenomena were ultimately reducible to some transformation of drive, i.e. sexual impulses (cf Greenberg, 1991). "Love" was seen as derivative of the sexual drive, libido. In Freud's later ego psychology, the goal is that the ego, ideally, works with the defenses to transform sexual impulses to allow for gratification in compromise with the requirements of the superego and what is feasible within the constraints imposed by reality, the external world.

These days, the ability to love might be formulated as involving care about the welfare of an other (cf Fromm, 1956), as well as mutuality and respect (cf Benjamin). We no longer require such a thorough-going adherence to drive theory, as did Freud and his followers.

What about work? Now we are in the realm of ego psychology. Freudian ego psychologists carved out a space distinct from the drive-defense area in which all psychic life was derived from conflict between these two elements. This they accomplished almost by fiat, by nominating a psychic "conflict-free sphere". This was a sphere in which ego functioning and rationality dominated, uncontaminated by the irrational forces of the drives (the id) and internalized prohibitions (the supergo). Among the defenses, sublimation dominated, enabled by energy cleansed of its not-necessarily adaptive aims, turned into more adaptive, functional ends, like learning and problem-solving. When conflict intruded into this space, ego functions were prone to disruption, as in the case of learning disorders.

To love and to work: to find a space for the play of libidinal energy, and to find a space for the unimpeded operation of ego functioning. This healthy state provided a safe space for fantasy, in the form of imagination, to fuel and guide the trajectories of development and change. Imagination is related to fantasy, perhaps denuded of libidinal elements, fantasy in a conflict-free sphere, one might say.

These days there are people who come to therapy or analysis because of blockages in the realms of love and/or work. They want to be in a relationship but feel blocked from developing a relationship; they are too anxious to go out and meet people, they lack self-confidence, there's always something wrong with the people they meet. In such cases, exploring conflict or blocks around sexuality might seem like a promising road to explore to help such people. On the other hand, as Mitchell pointed out, the problem might lie with a difficulty choosing a path through life. With what kind of person, do I expect to feel most myself, most like my true self? Such people can benefit from being enabled to ask such questions.

11 Ankhi Mukherjee's Unseen City

Ankhi Mukherjee is exemplary as a contributor from an adjacent discipline who made a transformative contribution to psychoanalysis. As a literary scholar, and one who hails from India, she inherits Freud's creative legacy without the burden and baggage of the medical/scientific imperatives that came with, and continue to constrain, the field, theoretically and clinically.

The title of Ankhi Mukherjee's book says it all about Community Psychoanalysis. "Unseen" refers to the potential see-er, but the one who shuts down, the one who looks away. That's also what psychoanalysis is about: not seeing, looking away, repression, dissociation. However it is formulated, the psychoanalytic process is about rediscovery and recovery of what had long ago been relegated to the unseen and the processes by which that remains unseen. And what is that? In this case, a city, the postcolonial, cosmopolitan city: London, New York, Lagos, Chennai, and Mumbai. On the cover of the book is a cityscape photo consisting of tall, brightly lit buildings, highly visible, and the subject matter: the psychic lives of the urban poor. That signals a topic that can be uncomfortable, provoke guilt and anxiety.

The city where you live, along with the people who live there with you, but unseen. You will open your eyes to what you unknowingly had gone to great lengths *not* to see, the people just outside your door, perhaps living in economic poverty, homeless, unnoticed, in pain.

"Not seeing" is at the core of Sullivan's (1953) concept of "selective inattention".

Mukherjee's "unseen" sounds like selective inattention, but in fact it is more like what is now called "dissociation". Dissociated content is present in consciousness but without affect and without associative connections. People can speak of things that are dissociated, like childhood abuse or violent experiences, but in a weirdly disconnected way. To illustrate Mukherjee's "unseen": people who live in New York's affluent suburbs can drive daily through parts of the city that look "bombed out", home to thousands and millions of suffering people, all the while only thinking about personal concerns, small even in the personal scheme of things.

I am most drawn to Mukherjee's description of the research that led to her book as a form of "traveling psychoanalysis" (p. 211). This phrase captures

DOI: 10.4324/9781003661146-12

the essence of Community Psychoanalysis, in contrast to "office-based" psychoanalysis. When one travels, one enters into other people's worlds. One "*listens*". That's what most appeals to me about working out of my office. When the other enters my office, they enter my world, one way or another. They listen to me.

The historical backdrop to the sort of dissociation described just above is to be found in Robert Caro's (1974) biography of Robert Moses entitled *The Power Broker*. Robert Moses, in the early-to-mid twentieth century, was an unelected man with a dream, a dream of transforming the New York City-Long Island area with a vast system of parks and superhighways to connect them with the population center of New York City. Moses started with a network of parkways on Long Island, carefully woven around the palatial estates of the industrialist robber barons so as not to impinge upon them. Cultivating the favor of politicians wielding the power of the purse, such as Governor Alfred Smith, Moses financed his parkway projects as appointed Chairman of Parkway Authorities, non-governmental entities with access to government funding. Moses obtained access to public funding by immersing himself in the design and wording of legislation controlling such things as the use of revenue from bridge tolls and his own responsibilities as Chairman of a public authority. Thus equipped, operating largely out of public view, Moses created a positive image in the media as promoter of parks and recreation, and an efficient transportation system that was a marvel of the world. The reality was not noticed, that he arranged highways to make his parks accessible only with great difficulty to those who needed them most. The press created acclaim for Moses as the genius behind the great system of bridges, tunnels, and highways of the New York metropolitan area. Meanwhile, the rundown playgrounds of the Bronx and other such economically besieged communities remained unchanged. Moses totally neglected public transportation so that his exquisite parks were accessible only to the privileged few who owned cars, completely inaccessible to the masses of New York City residents who most needed them. Since Moses was appointed, unelected, the people who were excluded from the beaches and greenery of Long Island could not register a protest at the ballot box. Without the consent of the taxpaying residents of New York City and State, funding sources for expansion were tenuously maintained by the good favor of politicians who were pleased by the idealizing attention of the press and the construction jobs Moses could bestow on their constituents, especially during the Depression years.

Turning to New York City itself, Moses hit upon a new funding source: tolls paid to cross bridges. Without extensive public transportation, the Long Island parks could not be reached from Manhattan without bridges to carry motor vehicles. Moses manipulated the levers of government power to establish himself as the Chair of authorities such as the Triborough Bridge and Tunnel authority which made Long Island, Brooklyn, and Queens accessible to the car owners of Manhattan and New Jersey, and the tolls collected to the "authority" for building more bridges and highways without governmental authorization for the most part. The availability of highways, bridges, and tunnels enticed more people to buy cars, which in turn created more need for highways, bridges, and tunnels, which in turn generated more revenue for Moses's authorities. For Robert Moses, it was a dream come true.

Moses cared about motor vehicles, cars, and trucks, not people *per se*, especially the economically poor who did not own cars. Moses's inattention to economically poor people became consequential when he turned his attention to connecting New Jersey with Long Island via a new highway, the Cross Bronx Expressway. This expressway required displacement of tens of thousands of economically impoverished residents of the Bronx. A vast integrated suburbia took shape, a model for the nation, with people living in disconnected private houses, needing private cars (and fossil fuel) to go anywhere.

Caro details the heartlessness with which Moses destroyed the homes of many thousands of residents of the Bronx as he cleared the way for the Cross Bronx Expressway, along with other highways in New York City. In some cases, Caro documents how many buildings could have been spared, along with the homes of many people, by shifting the path of the highway a short distance to the right or the left. People whose homes were slated to be torn down were assured that new homes would be provided. When they followed instructions for how to access new homes, however, they were most often turned away. These were not just any people, however; they were people who lacked the resources to challenge their displacement in court. When it came to the estates of the "robber barons" of Long Island, however, parkways twisted and turned to avoid infringing on their property. Further suffering was imposed on many recent immigrants to the United States, who already were struggling to make a go of life in their new country. In the end, Moses was brought down when he tried to destroy trees near the homes of well-to-do residents of Central Park West in Manhattan to make way for a luxury restaurant, Tavern on the Green. When people went to court to try to prevent the degradation of the park in their front yard, the press in New York finally took notice. When Moses tried to cut down trees at night to avoid a court order ordering him not to do so, as he had been able to do with impunity in the Bronx, he lost the support of the Governor at the time, Nelson Rockefeller.

It became clear that if Robert Moses was heartless, he was heartless specifically in the cases of people who lacked the economic capacity to oppose him. The media, the courts, and the political establishment went along for the ride. The selective inattention of the well-to-do commuting through the South Bronx excluded not only the burned-out buildings but the shattered lives of their residents and the political processes that allowed all this to happen.

Psychoanalysis and other approaches to the alleviation of human suffering selectively restricted its focus and attention to the intrapsychic world. Some of the ways in which suffering was produced and reinforced socially-systemically were ruled out of the domain of psychoanalysis and other forms of psychotherapy, as it was ruled out of the domain of psychiatry with its attention restricted to the chemistry of the production of human suffering. Community Psychoanalysis seeks to widen the lens, making the "unseen city", along with the mechanisms of its perpetuation, more visible to those inclined to see.

Varieties of Truth: Literary Truth

Mukherjee's point of entry to the lives of the residents of the unseen city is sometimes by direct experience, sometimes by way of literature, via fiction produced by those who live in otherwise unseen places.

Fiction straddles the fence between objective reality and fantasy, like "fantasy" itself.

Freud's approach to truth straddles the fence between objective truth and subjective truth, a variation of which is what we might call "meaning". Meaning is an ambiguous and multi-faceted word, the meaning of which goes far beyond dictionary-type definitions, as in "this means that". No: meaning gets into the realm of meaning as in "meaningful", or "worthwhile", or "that has meaning to me". Meaning emerges when something gets attached to feelings or experiences of value. Meaning emerges when words or other symbols are a starting point for personal associations or trains of personal associations. Ultimately, Freud attempted a balancing act, tried to segregate "meaning" into the realm of dreams, or free association on the couch, without abandoning the objective truth which was the stock in trade of scientists and medical doctors.

The fact that words, alone or in combination with other words, always have meaning in excess of the literal dictionary meanings of words powers the change potential in talk therapies. We never quite know, definitively, what we are saying, or what we might be heard to say or what someone might associate with what we say. The horizon of meaning expands and shifts in unpredictable ways when we talk or when we listen. The indeterminacy of meaning in words, not just in poetry, leaves plenty of room for imagination, creativity, and thus change.

When the case study becomes "fiction" (which also, colloquially, means "not true", from a rigid point of view in which "true" and "false" are split off from each other), these categories must be rethought.

Metaphorical truth, however, is a different species of truth, the stock in trade of literary fiction and psychoanalysis. In an objectivist framework, the boundary between external reality and internal reality is clearly and unambiguously demarcatable, so that the truth or falsity of a proposition is determinable regardless of the perspective of the speaker. In a relativistic framework, in physical sciences like pre-relativity physics, as in social sciences like psychology, the perspective of the observer matters. What is true from one perspective may or may not be true from another. Nonetheless, not everything goes. There is a large and complex gray area, owing to the human capacity to take account of another's perspective, even to adopt the perspective of another, at least provisionally, once it is explained. On this basis, all forms of negotiation, and psychotherapy, become possible.

An even more gray area appears when one considers the realm of poetry, or psychoanalytic "free association", or dreams. Here is the domain Freud entered in works such as *The Interpretation of Dreams*. (Freud, 1900) Freud attempted to make dreams legible by positing a different logic, "primary process" he called it, and a guide to translating from one system of logic to the other, back and forth between ordinary waking Aristotelian logic, and what Freud called "primary process" logic.

To take one example: in primary process logic, one thing can represent its opposite. As another example, the President of the United States can represent the dreamer's father (or mother). Once we cut loose from Aristotelian logic, the relationship between subjective (psychic) reality and objective (external) reality becomes quite slippery. This aspect of psychoanalysis accounts for a good deal of skepticism, if not ridicule, among members of the general public. But, as an analyst, I must point out that there is a danger of the baby getting thrown out with the bathwater.

Cutting loose from objectivism risks feeling at sea. With no concrete, i.e. physical, place, to hold on to for a sense of security, it can feel that anything goes, that there's no way to distinguish between the baby and the bathwater. The fear of feeling adrift is a major liability for psychoanalysis. Putting oneself in the hands of a psychoanalyst can feel like entrusting oneself to a cult leader.

The fact is, however, that in the "hard" sciences too, the meaning of quantitative data, the most seemingly unambiguous data, is also up for grabs, subject to interpretation. That is why, in the medical sciences, treatment recommendations are revised every few years, sometimes based on new data, to be sure, but sometimes also based on new studies, new ways of thinking, or interpreting data.

In courts of law, where so much is at stake in judgments as to whether a narrative is true "beyond a reasonable doubt" or true by virtue of a "preponderance of evidence", different standards apply. Even in scientific studies, statistics are used (arbitrarily) to estimate the likelihood that a conclusion is wrong. Do you want a conclusion that is justified at the .01 level or the .05 level? And how will you balance that with an arbitrarily selected degree of power?

The problem with literary-type interpretation, however, is of an entirely different order (or is it?). Consider the following stanza from Robert Frost's poem, "Stopping by Woods on a Snowy Evening":

The woods are lovely, dark, and deep, but I have promises to keep,
And miles to go before I sleep
And miles to go before I sleep.

(Frost, 2001)

World weary! But who doesn't have promises to keep? The repetition of this phrase enacts the trudging action, putting one foot in front of the other, as the snow slowly swirls. The deep dark midnight forest seems to offer a refuge; the poet on his horse pauses, thinking how nice it would be to lie down and rest—-but life with its endless tasks calls, and he keeps slowly, deliberately, moving.

How profound is the truth evoked by these words, via images and associations! But what kind of truth is that? A single word, "truth" on a number of levels, points to something fundamental about life and living, while also informing his (evidence-based) choice as to which path to take at the upcoming crossroads, to reach the village where he can keep his promises. Multiple forms of truth intersect, enriching each other.

The value of an interpretation like this depends on the imaginative resonance it evokes between and among different people. Freud proposed rules for transformation from symbol to symbol, from image to image, that could systematize communication in the language of primary process. He gave no evidence of thinking of these rules as culturally specific. Symbols with universal or cross-cultural resonance, like death in the Frost poem above. Death, never having been experienced by hardly anyone, can *only* be imaginatively constructed.

Likewise love, which is one word with many deeply personal meanings, so that each individual is thrown back on hardly verbalizable experiences in order to make meaning of the word. Likewise loss.

These domains of experience are studied only by stretching objectifying methods almost or beyond the breaking point.

The value of literary presentation of experience can be judged by aesthetic quality and the capacity to enrich and illuminate life experience via metaphor, like poetry. Using literary means to evoke or produce experience may be therapeutic in powerfully documenting and sharing the experience of suffering, especially for those who are inclined to minimize or disqualify the validity of their experience. Literary means can produce and reinforce the experience of having a voice, both for the author and for those who identify with the author. Literary means, however, do not necessarily expose the inequities and injustices that produce and perpetuate unhappiness. Like psychotherapy and psychoanalysis itself, the narrow lens ignores the social and political enabling forces. No particular medium, from fiction to journalism, can accomplish all purposes at once. But a disinclination to see what has been wrought is produced and reinforced by the media, especially in the age of mass produced, mass-consumed media that has the capacity to influence public consciousness profoundly and pervasively. For those inclined to blame themselves for their suffering (Sennett & Cobb, 1972), fiction can illuminate all at once the socio-political context, e.g. racial discrimination, immigration, and the counterproductive individually based elements, e.g. "learned helplessness" (Seligman & Maier, 1967) and substance abuse. "Unseen City" creates a crack in a heavily reinforced armor of denial and obscurantism.

Even within the narrow world of psychoanalytic and psychotherapeutic theory and practice, the narrowing of the lens has problematic consequences. For example, the individual focus of much psychotherapy has the potential to reinforce "blame the victim" dynamics, while a one sided focus on social oppression can reinforce learned helplessness on the individual level. Fiction can bring these diverse levels together in an experientially evocative way, bypassing abstract, intellectual, theoretical tangles.

The novels of Franz Kafka provide powerful examples of the illuminating power of fiction. Consider *Metamorphosis* (Kafka, 1915). Kafka's story of a man who wakes up to discover he has turned into a cockroach. Thinking metaphorically, this story will resonate with many of us who have felt like a degraded pest. Another story, *The Trial* is about a man who is evidently accused of having committed a crime, the details of which are never made clear, but for which he is nonetheless being held accountable in an official court of law. This story captures the experience of being haunted by guilt, pervasive yet without clearly defined origin. No clinical summary, complete with ICD-10 or DSM-V diagnosis and associated evidence-based treatment plan could capture the uncanny, haunting quality evoked by these stories. When the problem or dysfunction is defined in observable, measurable, terms there is an advantage in the clarity thus achieved. There is a reassuringly definitive quality to the assessment of what is wrong, and how it can be fixed, that leaves little room for uncertainty. But something important is lost as well: imagination.

Conclusion

So where do we stand in efforts to preserve and protect what is valuable in psychoanalysis while being open to updating the theory and practice to make psychoanalysis more accessible and useful to a wider range of people in a diverse and fast-changing world?

Some analysts, to be sure, can only imagine psychoanalysis in a traditionally "proper" frame. Others reconsider what constitutes a proper frame, such that it can encompass both office-based and out-of-office-based works, or in-office but face to face, or at lesser frequency. One also sees reconsideration of therapeutic action, beyond cognitive and verbally based insight, so as to expand criteria for analyzability to become more relational, and thereby more culturally and socioeconomically inclusive. I do not assume that whatever is thought to account for therapeutic change is all that's going on in any particular analytic moment. The analyst may be aiming not only at insight but a new emotional experience, or some other potentially mutative factor may be operative under the radar of one or both parties. The analyst may be busy trying to foster some sort of insight, while the patient may be most focused on small kindnesses that slip out from under the analyst's well-rehearsed demeanor.

There is much of value in psychoanalysis, in the psychoanalytic legacy, that I don't want us to lose. I hope that Community Psychoanalysis can maintain its connection with a psychoanalytic way of listening to what is spoken and to what is unspoken. I also hope that Community Psychoanalysis can avoid losing its way in misguided efforts to establish its psychoanalytic credentials with unnecessary extrinsic technical rigidities and criteria for being a "good" patient, based on a one-sided emphasis on verbal and cognitive capacities associated with a particular educational background.

Freud (1912) wrote that any treatment addressing transference and resistance is essentially psychoanalysis. Adding "countertransference" to this list updates the definition by taking account of the recent relational turn. No mention was made of a private office setting, nor of any office setting, for that matter; no mention is made of a couch, of frequency of sessions, of abstinence or anonymity. That said, I suggest that what has been called

DOI: 10.4324/9781003661146-13

"Community Psychoanalysis" in this book can validly be called, straight up, "psychoanalysis". Until the in-office setting was ruled out during the COVID pandemic, classical psychoanalytic organizations like the American Psycho-analytic Association insisted on the longer list of criteria (sometimes called "extrinsic") for a treatment to be considered "psychoanalytic". With the limitations imposed by the pandemic, psychoanalysts practicing exclusively in-office were at risk of becoming unemployed, underemployed, and even extinct. Under those conditions, the tentatively accepted category of "Com-munity Psychoanalysis" moved toward the mainstream. Freud's definition of "psychoanalysis", with the amendments discussed just above, could now stand without qualification. Many details still need to be worked out about defining and addressing transference, countertransference, and resistance in and out of the private office, forming the *raison d'etre* of this book.

Concerning both the frame and criteria for analyzability: I hope to have demonstrated that faithfulness to a set of outdated scientific principles, meant to ensure objectivity, has led the study of the human mind, by human beings, into a conundrum. Sigmund Freud, seeking to advance his revolutionary insights about psychic life in the face of powerful headwinds of scientific orthodoxy and antisemitism, left us a brilliantly creative legacy of psychoana-lytic theory and practice.

In this study of the evolution of psychoanalysis in the European-influenced world, we find that the notion of objectivity, the separation of subject and object in a "proper" scientific study, was a guiding principle for Freud and his followers. In the abstract realm of theory, this subject-object split seemed straightforward enough, but when Freud applied his ideas to clinical practice, he ran into complications and obstacles. To his credit, when he ran into complications and obstacles, Freud took them as spurs to further think-ing. Meanwhile, some analysts, whether they identify as analysts or not, have been experimenting with doing psychoanalysis, by their lights, in a variety of settings.

Freud (1927) was, as usual, way ahead of his time, in noting, seemingly off-handedly, that an education in the humanities was perhaps the best prepa-ration for working as an analyst. We noted a similar point in discussing the way "meaning" takes shape in language. The dictionary-definition of words, as we noted, obscures the indeterminacy of word-meaning, even of single words, and we're not even talking about poetry. The range of meanings float-ing around words leaves plenty of room for creativity and play in even fairly straightforward sentences. Thus enters the unconscious in everyday life!

There are many strands woven into the tapestry of Community Psychoa-nalysis. Being more flexible about the frame is an important thread that I have returned to repeatedly in this book, but there is more: group dynamics, group defenses, inclusion of the arts and literature, ways of doing politics and inter-national relations, ways of doing business. We don't want to be so inclusive that "psychoanalysis" loses any specific meaning. Yet we also want to avoid so much specificity that we lose sight of what psychoanalysis can contribute to so much of what we do.

I will conclude with some reflections on "the frame", the setup, that makes effective psychoanalytic work possible. I hope to have demonstrated that, early on, abstinence, anonymity, and neutrality (defined at that point as equidistance between id, ego, and superego) took center stage in guiding conceptions of the ideal frame. Underlying the selection of these qualities were ideals of scientific objectivity, non-exploitation of the patient sexually and otherwise, and an over-riding focus on the patient's experience and feelings. Over the decades it has become apparent that, while these objectives may be important and facilitative of an analytic process, it is impossible and undesirable, counterproductive in fact, to bend too far in the opposite direction. We risk falling over backward if we rigidly eliminate, or even attempt to eliminate, the analyst's subjective experience, intuition, and feelings.

Rather, the goal should be redefined as subordinating understanding and articulation of the analyst's feelings and experience to understanding and articulating the patients' feelings and experience, and how they arise in the interaction between the two (or more) people involved. The analyst is called on to feel and to think *and* to think about how his or her feelings and thoughts arise in this particular interaction. Doing this work with the patient helps to build skills for the patient to use in the analysis and beyond. Lying on the couch, frequency of sessions, intentional disclosure of the analyst's own experience, location of the session in an office or in the street, with a high fee or low, all these things and more can be thought about in terms of whether they are likely to advance or impede the above-mentioned purposes (and we are never sure), not in a one-size-fits-all mechanical or prescribed effort to achieve objectivity or neutrality.

It is high time to do justice to the full range of inclusive values that analysts in fact hold. In pursuit of efforts to make psychoanalysis more broadly acces-sible, flexibility in the frame (with respect to location in which the analytic work takes place, with whom it takes place, perhaps inclusive of the social third, mindful of the analyst's complex, multi-layered, and shifting subjectiv-ity) might be necessary and advisable. All this means that what takes place within the frame will more closely resemble real life and thus more relevant to real life. This book has tracked halting efforts to move in this direction, mindful of commitments and values (scientific- and social justice-related) that have been there all along, but not always honored.

References

Altman, N. (1995) *The Analyst in the Inner City: Race, Class and Culture through a Psychoanalytic Lens*. Hillsdale, NJ: The Analytic Press.

Altman, N. (2010) *The Analyst in the Inner City: Race, Class and Culture through a Psychoanalytic Lens*. Second Edition. New York and London: Routledge.

Altman, N. (2015) *Psychoanalysis in an Age of Accelerating Cultural Change: Spiritual Globalization*. New York and London: Routledge.

Altman, N. (2024) What's Not Uncanny? *Contemporary Psychoanalysis*. 60:1–15. https://doi.org/10.1080/00107530.2024.2397312

Alvarez, A. (1992) *Live Company*. London and New York: Routledge & Kegan Paul.

Baldwin, J. (1962) Letter to my nephew on the one hundredth anniversary of the emancipation. In: *The Fire Next Time*. pp. 3–10. New York: Dial Press.

Bass, A. (2007) When the frame doesn't fit the picture. *Psychoanalytic Dialogues*. 17:1–28.

Beebe, B., Cohen, P., Sossin, M. & Markese, S. (Eds.) (2012) *Mothers, Infants and Young Children of September 11, 2001: A Primary Prevention Project*. New York: Routledge.

Beebe, B., Knoblauch, S., Rustin, J. & Sorter, D. (2005) *Forms of Intersubjectivity in Infant Research and Adult Treatment*. New York: Other Press.

Beebe, B. & Lachmann, F. (2002) *Infant Research and Adult Treatment: Co-Constructing Interactions*. Hillsdale, NJ: Analytic Press.

Beebe, B., Lachmann, F. & Cohen, P. (2016) *The Mother-Infant Interaction Picture Book: Origins of Attachment*. New York: Norton.

Benjamin, J. (2004) Doer and done to: an intersubjective view of thirdness. *Psychoanalytic Quarterly*. 73:5–46.

Berlin, I. (1969) *Four Essays on Liberty*. Oxford: Oxford University Press.

Bersani, L. (2002) *Introduction to Freud, S. Civilization and Its Discontents*. A. Phillips, ed. London and New York: Penguin Books.

Bion, W.R. (1987) *Experiences in Groups*. London: Routledge.

Bion, W.R. (1988) Attacks on linking. In: E. Bott-Spillius (Ed.) *Melanie Klein Today*. Vol. 1, pp. 87–101. London: Routledge and Kegan Paul.

Bodnar, S. (2006) I'm in the milk and the milk's in me: Eros in the clinical relationship. *Psychoanalytic Dialogues*. 16(1):45–68.

Bragin, M. (2005) Pedrito: exploring the riots if aggression through the traditional treatment of a former child soldier in Angola. *Journal of Infant, Child, and Adolescent Psychotherapy*. 4:1–21.

Brenman-Pick, I. (1985/1988) Working through in the counter-transference. In: E.B. Spillius (Ed.) *Melanie Klein Today*, Vol. 2. pp. 34–47. London: Routledge.

Britton, R. (1992) The oedipus situation and the depressive position. In: R. Anderson (Ed.) *Clinical Lectures on Klein and Bion*. pp. 34–45. London: Routledge.

Caro, R. (1974) *The Power Broker: Robert Moses and the Fall of New York*. New York: Knopf.

Cohen, A., Patel, V. & Minas, H. (2013) A brief history of global mental health. In: V. Patel, H. Minas, A. Cohen, & M. Prince (Eds.) *Global Mental Health: Principles and Practice*. Oxford: Oxford University Press.

Coles, R. (1967) *The Political Life of Children*. New York: Atlantic Monthly Press.

Coles, R. (2007) *The Moral Life of Children*. New York: Random House.

Dalal, F. (2002) *Race, Colour, and the Processes of Socialization. New Perspectives from Group Analysis, Psychoanalysis, Sociology*. New York: Brunner-Routledge.

Danto, E. (2005) *Freud's Free Clinics*. New York: Columbia University Press.

Davids, F. (2011) *Internal Racism: A Psychoanalytic Approach to Race and Difference*. New York: Red Globe Press.

Dewey, J. (1938) *Experience and Education*. New York: MacMillan.

Einstein, A. (1988) *Relativity: The Special and General Theories: A Clear Explanation That Anyone Can Understand*. New York and London: Routledge.

Elias, N. (1994) *The Civilizing Process*. Oxford: Blackwell.

Emmanuel, R. (1996) Psychotherapy traumatized in infancy. *Journal of Child Psychotherapy*. 22(2):214–239.

Erikson, E.H. (1968) *Identity, Youth, and Crisis*. New York: Norton.

Esprey, Y. (2017) The problem of thinking in black and white: race in the South African clinical dyad. *Psychoanalytic Dialogues*. 27(1): 20–35.

Fairbairn, W.R.D. (1952) *Psychoanalytic Studies of the Personality*. London: Routledge and Kegan Paul.

Fanon, F. (1963) *The Wretched of the Earth*. Hillsdale, NJ: Grove Press.

Felix, A. (2014) Violence and trauma among the homeless. In: C. Christian, M. Tolpin, & J. A. Anderson (Eds.) *Analysts in the Trenches: A Psychoanalytic Model for Change*. pp. 21–42. Hillsdale, NJ: The Analytic Press.

Ferenczi, S. (1933) Confusion of tongues between adults and the child. In: *Final Contributions to the Problems and Methods of Psycho-Analysis*. pp. 156–167. London: Hogarth, 1955.

Fonagy, P., Gergely, G., Jurist, E.L., & Target, M. (2002) *Affect Regulation, Mentalization, and the Self*. New York: Other Press.

Foucault, M. (1980) *The History of Sexuality*. (Vol.1) New York: Vintage.

Foulkes, S.H. & Anthony, E.J. (1957) *Group Psychotherapy—the Psychoanalytic Approach*. London: Karnac Books.

Freire, P. (1972) *The Pedagogy of the Oppressed*. London: Penguin.

Freud, A. (1966) *The Ego and the Mechanisms of Defense*. New York: International Universities Press.

Freud, A. (1989) *Normality and Pathology in Childhood: Assessments of Development*. New York: International Universities Press.

Freud, S. (1900) The interpretation of dreams. In J. Strachey (Ed. & Trans.) *The Standard Edition of the Complete Psychological Works of Sigmund Freud*. Vol. 4–5. London: Hogarth Press.

Freud, S. (1905) Three essays on the theory of sexuality. In: J. Strachey (Ed. & Trans.) *The Standard p of the Complete Psychological Works of Sigmund Freud*. Vol. 7, pp. 123–246. London: Hogarth Press.

Freud, S. (1919) Lines of advance in psychoanalytic therapy. In: J. Strachey (Ed. & Trans.) *The Complete Psychological Works of Sigmund Freud*. Vol. 7, pp. 125–245. London: Hogarth Press.

Freud, S. (1920) *Beyond the Pleasure Principle*. Standard Edition, Vol. 18, pp. 1–64. London: Hogarth Press.

Freud, S. (1921) *Mass Psychology and Analysis of the Ego*. London: Hogarth Press.

Freud, S. (1933/1964) Dissecting the psychical personality. In: J. Strachey (Ed. & Trans.) *The Complete Psychological Works of Sigmund Freud*. Vol. 22, pp. 59–80. London: Hogarth Press.

Freud, S. (1937) Analysis terminable and interminable. In: J. Strachey (Ed. & Trans.) *The Complete Psychological Works of Sigmund Freud*. Vol. 23, pp. 216–253. London: Hogarth Press.

Freud, S. (2002) *Civilization and Its Discontents*. (D. McClintock, Trans.) London: Penguin.

Fromm, E. (1941) *Escape from Freedom*. New York: Farrar & Rinehart.

Fromm, E. (1956) *The Art of Loving*. New York: Harper.

Fromm-Reichmann, F. (1960) *Principles of Intensive Psychotherapy*. Chicago: University of Chicago Press.

Frost, R. (2001) *Stopping by Woods on a Snowy Evening*. New York: Penguin Young Readers.

Gabbard, G.O. (1986) The treatment of the "special" patient in a psychoanalytic hospital. *International Review of Psychoanalysis*. 13:333–347.

Gaztambide, D. (2024) *Decolonizing Psychoanalytic Technique: Putting Freud on Fanon's Couch*. London: Palgrave MacMillan.

Ghent, E. (1990) Paradox and process. *Psychoanalytic Dialogues*. 1(1):35–54.

Ghent, E. (1991) Masochism, submission, surrender: masochism as a perversion of surrender. *Contemporary Psychoanalysis*. 27(1):108–136.

Gill, M. (1983) *Analysis of Transference* volume 1. New York: International Universities Press.

Gleick, J. (2011) *Chaos: Making a New Science*. New York: Viking Books.

Greenberg, J. & Mitchell, S.A. (1983) *Object Relations in Psychoanalytic Theory*. Cambridge, MA: Harvard University Press.

Greenberg, J. (1991) *Oedipus and beyond*. Cambridge, MA and London: Harvard University Press.

Guttman, S.A. (1961) Panel reports: criteria for analyzability. *Journal of the American Psychoanalytic Association*. 8:141–151.

Harris, A. (2005) *Gender as Soft Assembly*. Hillsdale, NJ: The Analytic Press.

Hegel, G.W.F. (1807) *The Phenomenology of Spirit*. Hamburg: Felix Meiner.

Hoffman, I. Z. (1983) The patient as interpreter of the analyst's experience. *Contemporary Psychoanalysis* 19:389–422.

Hoffman, I.Z. (1998) *Ritual and Spontaneity in the Psychoanalytic Process*. Hillsdale, NJ: The Analytic Press.

Jacoby, R. (1983) *The Repression if Psychoanalysis*. New York: Basic Books.

Jones, E. (1953) *The Life and Work of Sigmund Freud Vol. 1 The Formative Years and the Great Discoveries. 1856-1900*. New York: Basic Books.

Joseph, B. (1998) Thinking about a playroom. *Journal of Child Psychotherapy.* 24(3):359–366.

Kafka, F. (1915) *The Metamorphosis.* New York: Norton.

Kernberg, O. (1992) *Aggression in Personality Disorders and Perversions.* New Haven, CT: Yale University Press.

Kita, E. (2019) They hate me now, but where were they when I needed them?: mass incarceration, projective identification, and Social Work praxis. *Psychoanalytic Social Work.* 26:1 25–49.

Klein, M. (1952) Some theoretical conclusions regarding the emotional life of the infant. In: R. Money-Kyrle (Ed.) *The Writings of Melanie Klein.* Vol. 8, pp. 61–94. London: Envy and Gratitude and Other Works, Hogarth Press.

Kliman, G. (2011) *Reflective Network Therapy in the Preschool Classroom.* Lanham, MD: Rowman Littlefield.

Kohut, H. (1977) *The Restoration of the Self.* New York: International Universities Press.

Kraemer, S.B. (2006) So the cradle won't fall: holding the staff who hold the parents in the NICU. *Psychoanalytic Dialogues.* 16(2):149–164.

Kraemer, S.B. & Steinberg, Z. (2006) It's rarely cold in the NICU: the permeability of psychic space. *Psychoanalytic Dialogues.* 16(2):165–179.

Kurtz, S. (1977) *The Art of Unknowing: Dimensions of Openness in Analytic Therapy.* Northvale, NJ: Jason Aronson.

Lacan, J. (1978) *The Four Fundamental Concepts of Psychoanalysis.* (Jacques-Alain Miller, ed., Alan Sheridan, tr.) New York: Norton.

Laing, R.D. & Esterson, A. (1970) *Sanity, Madness, and the Family.* Hammondsworth, Middlesex, England: Penguin.

Langer, M. (1989) *From Vienna to Managua: Journey of a Psychoanalyst.* London: Free Association Press.

Lasch, P. (1979) *The Culture of Narcissism: American Life in an Age of Diminishing Expectations.* New York: Norton.

Levenson, E. (1972) *The Fallacy of Understanding.* New York: Basic Books.

Lipton, S.D. (1979) The advantages of Freud's technique as shown in his analysis of the Rat Man. *International Journal of Psychoanalysis.* 58:255–274.

Loewald, H. (1988) *Sublimation.* New Haven, CT: Yale University Press.

Main, T. (1957) The ailment. *British Journal of Medical Psychology.* 30(3–4):129–145, Reprinted in: Main, T.F. (1989) *The Ailment and Other Psychoanalytic Essays.* London: Free Association Books.

Malberg, N. (2008) Refusing to be excluded: finding ways of integrating psychotherapeutic modalities to the emerging needs of a pupil referral unit. *Journal of Child Psychotherapy.* 34:101–110.

Martin-Baro, I. (1994) *Writings for a Liberation Psychology.* Cambridge, MA: Harvard University Press.

Melville, H. (1929) *Moby Dick.* New York: MacMillan.

Menzies-Lyth, I.E.P. (1975) A case study in the functioning of social systems as a defense against anxiety. In: A. D. Colman and W. H. Bexton (Eds.) *Group Relations Reader.* Vol. 1, pp.281–312. Jupiter, FL: A.K. Rice Institute.

Mitchell, S.A. (1988) *Relational Concepts in Psychoanalysis.* Cambridge, MA: Harvard University Press.

Mitchell, S.A. (1993) *Hope and Dread in Psychoanalysis.* New York: Basic Books.

Mitchell, S.A. (1997) *Influence and Autonomy in Psychoanalysis*. Hillsdale, NJ: The Analytic Press.

Mukherjee, A. (2022) *Unseen City: The Psychic Lives of the Urban Poor*. Cambridge: Cambridge University Press.

Music, G. & Hall, B. (2008) From scapegoating to thinking and finding a home: delivering therapeutic work in schools. *Journal of Child Psychotherapy*. 34(1):43–61.

Najmabadi, A. (2005) *Women with Mustaches and Men without Beards: Gender and Sexual Anxieties of Iranian Modernity*. Berkeley: University of California Press.

Nicholsen, S.W. (2002) *The Love of Nature and the End of the World*. Cambridge and London: The MIT Press.

Nunberg, H. (1932) *Address to the 1932 Nuremberg Congress of the International Psychoanalytical Association (IPA)*.

Ogden, T. (1986) *The Matrix of the Mind*. Northvale, NJ: Jason Aronson.

Ogden, T. (1994) *Subjects of Analysis*. Northvale, NJ: Jason Aronson.

Ogden, T. (2001) *Conversations at the Frontier of Dreaming*. Northvale, NJ: Jason Aronson.

Parker, R. (2019) Slavery in the white psyche. Psychoanalytic Social Work.

Phillips, A. (1993) *On Kissing, Tickling, and Being Bored*. Cambridge, MA: Harvard University Press.

Pine, F. (1985) *Developmental Theory and Clinical Process*. New Haven, CT: Yale University Press.

Pine, F. (1990) *Drive, Ego, Object, and Self: A Synthesis for Clinical Work*. New York: Basic Books.

Pizer, S. (1999) *Building Bridges: The Negotiation of Paradox in Psychoanalysis*. New York and London: Routledge.

Rotter, J.B. (1966) Generalized expectancies for internal versus external control of reinforcement. *Psychological Monographs*. 80:1–28.

Roy, A. (2024) *Intimacy in Alienation: A Psychoanalytic Study of Hindu-Muslim Relationships*. New Delhi: Yoda Press.

Sacco, F.C. & Twemlow, S.W. (1997) School violence reduction: A model Jamaican secondary school program. *Community Mental Health Journal*. 33(3):229–234. DOI: 10.1023/A:1025037527652

Sachdev, D. (2024) University as a temple: a psychoanalytic reflection on caste and education rituals. *American Imago*. 79(4):731–753.

Sacramone, A.M. (2012) Free association in the width of the square: building a model for developmental change from recognition and responsivity. *Presented at the International Association for Psychoanalytic Self Psychology conference*. Washington, DC. October 18, 2012.

Sarason, S.B., Levine, M., Goldenberg, I.I., Cherlin, D.L. & Bennett, D.L. (1966) *Psychology in Community Settings: Clinical, Educational, Vocational, Social Aspects*. New York: Wiley.

Sartre, J.P. (1993) *Being and Nothingness*. New York: Washington Square Press.

Searles, H. (1979) Unconscious processes in the environmental crisis. In: *Countertransference and Related Subjects*. pp. 228–242. New York: International Universities Press.

Seligman, M.E.P. & Meier, S.F. (1967) Failure to escape traumatic shock. *Journal of Experimental Psychology*. 74(1):1–9.

Sengupta, S. (2022) What fungi can teach us. *New York Times*: August 2, 2022.

Sennett, R. & Cobb, J. (1972) *The Hidden Injuries of Class*. New York: Vintage.

Shaw, D. (2013) *Traumatic Narcissism and Recovery*. New York and London: Routledge.

Sklarew, B., Twemlow, S.W., & Wilkinson, S.W. (2004) *Analysts in the Trenches: Streets, Schools, War Zones*. New York and London: Routledge.

Sprince, J. (2002) Developing containment: psychoanalytic consultancy to a therapeutic community for traumatized children. *Journal of Child Psychotherapy*. 28:2 147–161.

Stanton, A.H. & Schwartz, M.S. (1954) *The Mental Hospital*. New York: Basic Books.

Starr, K. & Aron, L. (2013) *A Psychotherapy for the People*. London and New York: Routledge.

Steinberg, Z. (2006) Pandora meets the NICU parent, or whither hope? *Psychoanalytic Dialogues*. 16(2):133–147.

Stern, D.B. (1997) *Unformulated Experience: From Dissociation to Imagination in Psychoanalysis*. Hillsdale, NJ: The Analytic Press.

Sullivan, H.S. (1953) *The Interpersonal Theory of Psychiatry*. New York: Norton

Thelen, E. & Smith, L.B. (1994) *A Dynamic Systems Approach to the Development of Cognition and Action*. Cambridge: MIT Press.

Twemlow, S.W. & Sacco, F.C. (1996) Peacekeeping and peacemaking: The conceptual foundations of a plan to reduce violence and improve the quality of life in a midsized community in Jamaica. *Psychiatry*. 59(2):156–174.

Twemlow, S. & Wilkinson, S. (2014) Topeka's healthy community initiative. In: B. Sklarew, S. W. Twemlow, & S. M. Wilkinson (Eds.) *Analysts in the Trenches: A Psychoanalytic Model for Change*. pp. 103–135. Hillsdale, NJ: The Analytic Press.

Vahali, H. (2009) *Lives in Exile: Exploring the Inner World if Tibetan Refugees*. New Delhi: Routledge.

Winnicott, D.W. (1952/1958) *Through Pediatrics to Psychoanalysis*. New York: Basic Books.

Winnicott, D.W. (1960/1965) Ego distortion in terms of true and false self. In: *The Maturational Processes and the Facilitating Environment*. pp. 140–152. New York: International Universities Press.

Winnicott, D.W. (1971) *Playing and Reality*. Harmondsworth, Middlesex, England: Penguin.

Wolfenstein, M. & Kliman, G. (Eds.) (1965) *Children and the Death of a President: Multi-Disciplinary Studies*. Garden City, NY: Doubleday.

Wordsworth, W. (1802) My heart leaps up. *Poem*.

Young-Bruehl, E. (2012) *Childism: Confronting Prejudice Against Children*. New Haven and London: Yale University Press.

Index

For Product Safety Concerns and Information please contact our EU
representative GPSR@taylorandfrancis.com
Taylor & Francis Verlag GmbH, Kaufingerstraße 24, 80331 München, Germany

www.ingramcontent.com/pod-product-compliance
Lightning Source LLC
Chambersburg PA
CBHW070350270326
41926CB00017B/4080

9 7 8 1 0 4 1 0 9 7 7 3 0